MW00886353

Confessions

of a

Former

Wall Street Whiz Kid

Fifth Edition

by Peter Grandich

with Jo Smith Schloeder
and John Archibald

Copyright © 2011-2021 Peter Grandich,
Jo Smith Schloeder (First through Third Edition)
and John Archibald (Fourth and Fifth Edition)

All rights reserved.

Author's Note:

Chapters 1 through 13 were written in 2011 as part of the first edition.

Chapter 14 was written in 2014 and released with the second edition.

Chapters 15 through 17 were written in 2015 and released with the third and fourth edition.

Chapters 18 and 19 were written in 2021 and released with the fifth edition.

Contents

Letters to Peter Grandich

In celebration of his 35th year in the financial services industry, the following four friends and past employers of Peter's provided these letters of congratulation for the release of this 5th edition.

Letter from Bob Knapp (Peter's first Wall Street employer 1984 – owned Brown & Knapp, Member, NYSE)

As I enter the twilight of my years, I look back on my life's experiences. In my retrospection, the one thing that I have realized is that life is full of surprises - some good and some bad. But, in all cases, I learned that we should "expect the unexpected".

One of my pleasant life's surprises came from the unexpected results of my hiring you as a stockbroker. Back then, a high school dropout stood before me looking for a break.

In those days, 35 years ago, we had hired two "types": the college grads who had rich relatives and college alumni contacts and the 'blue collar' types who would appeal to the "common man" and who "spoke his language".

The college grads had the "cushy" jobs of calling graduates from their school yearbooks and family members. The "blue collar" types had to perform boiler-room cold-calling. Coldcalling is a rigorous and frustrating necessity to unearth business.

You relentlessly went through the list of telephone numbers, suffered the hang-ups, the abuses and the indignities of those that you called and, undiscouraged, you continued to do your best to build a book of business. At first, I simply thought that you were a workaholic because, long after the rest of the office was long gone for the day, there you were working to build your book of business. But then I realized that you had a quality that the others did not embody: you believed in yourself and you believed in your message. You were a sincere professional working in an insincere, self-serving profession!

Peter, I knew that you would do well because you had such a way with the "common man" and "the elite". They were equals in your eyes and this was a part of your formula for success. And you had an altruistic calling – you simply wanted to help people to invest properly.

It's been especially gratifying to see you grow in your Christian Walk. When we first met, you knew little of our faith. But thanks to the Guardian Angel that God had sent you who was embodied in your wife, Mary. She was sent to you in order to help guide you to eternal life that now awaits you as a child of a Living God.

Stay the course of tying your faith to your work because I know all you have gone through was to be here as a Godly voice in an industry that's totally devoid of faith these days.

Letter from Bob Trause (Hired Peter in 1986, was Branch Manager for Philips, Appel & Walden and was an important person who helped to launch the "Wall Street Whiz Kid")

It's my pleasure to write about the "Wall Street Whiz Kid".

I am proud to have mentored Peter during his early years in the brokerage community and that I had contributed to his path in the investment profession. It is amazing that over 30 years has passed since that first day when I had interviewed this "diamond in the rough", who came to me with limited experience and a very small book of business. I hired him because I sensed a special quality and his success has only validated my "gut reaction" to hire Peter.

Back in October 1987, I can still recall Peter speaking of an impending stock market crash and the company's visceral reaction was to demand that he "retract it or else!"

A short time later, Black Monday (10/19/1987) hit leaving most completely unprepared – except those who took Peter seriously. Then, on the very next day, he announced his forecast that within two years that the stock market would make new, all-time highs! I was speechless!

My initial confusion was fed by the rhetorical question: "How could a young man who has had less than three years of professional accreditation possibly see clearly that which we all had missed?" His instinctive insight had me scratching what was left on top of my head. But, I had also learned an important "life's lesson" – in this business, we must always be circumspect and not have our instincts drowned-out by the shouting mob of like-thinking investors. So, for as much as I had taught Peter, he left me with a lesson to look at things with "new set of eyes" in this business.

Congratulations Peter! To think that I had played a role in your wonderful career is an honor. But I still believe that Mary had to have something to do with it as you would be lost without her!

Letter from Lou Scatigna, President of AFM Investments (Hired Peter in 1989. Some of Peter's fondest memories are due to both Lou, and his partner, Marty Saltzman)

It's my pleasure to say a few words about a man who taught me much and who I'm honored to call my friend.

For a man who had never even finished secondary education, Peter, you are living proof that formal education is not the only route to a well-earned, international recognition in matters of finance.

Your accomplishments are a testament to a man who believed in himself and who was not influenced by the "mob mentality" that is so typical of the financial products profession. You were always "your own man" and stayed your course - even when you were ridiculed and were "a lonely voice in the wilderness". Peter, you were typically and consistently "ahead of your time".

While I miss the days of your involvement in the metals and mining industry, I admire your desire to tie your faith to your work in an industry where that is rarely seen – or risked. Both my partner, and your friend, Marty Saltzman, and I wish you, Mary and Tara, many years of happiness and good health.

Always know that we are very grateful to have had you work with us. You made a difference in our personal lives, in our business, and in our professional lives.

Letter from Frank Congilose (First hired Peter in 2000. Peter's Financial Mentor and Peter's #1 trusted Financial Advisor)

Congratulations on your 35th anniversary in financial services.

Although I have hired and coached many people in my career, I clearly recall our first meeting 20 years ago. At the time that we had first met, you were dealing with some personal struggles and challenges. What I grew to appreciate and admire in you was how you always turned to your faith, family, and friends to help you through challenging times. They say the character of a man is seen not when he is doing great but when he is at his lowest point. Although I have seen you at a couple of low points over the years, I appreciate that you have never let those points in time define you. I am proud to have been and continue to be your friend and sounding board during the various stages of your personal and professional life.

I truly believe that God had used that time to mold you into the Godly man that you had become.

It is not easy tying one's faith to one's work, especially in our business. I congratulate you for living what Jesus said about not being able to serve both Him and money. Anyone, who has had the pleasure of knowing you, can easily see where you stand on that issue.

I'm honored whenever you tell people that I'm one of the very few people that you believe is both smart and honest in our business. You're not too shabby yourself!!

Acknowledgments

There are too many people to thank. So many people have contributed in one way or another to this book that I really should acknowledge no man. Yet, in this third edition, I'll point out one. As I enter my 13th and final year of doing Bible study and chapel services with the New York Giants, I would like to give special thanks to George McGovern, Team Chaplain, for allowing me to be part of the inner circle of professional sports. As I note in chapter 15, I believe George is an exemplary model of how a Christian man should live his life, and I am grateful for his friendship, wisdom and Christian example.

Finally, I am mindful that none of us would exist, let alone be owed a debt of gratitude, if it weren't for my Lord and Savior, Jesus Christ, providing the grace for all of us sinners. I only hope before my last breath that I have one pure moment of nothing on my mind but Jesus on the cross and what it has meant for all of existence now and forever.

—Peter Grandich
Freehold, New Jersey

14

Foreword

It's funny how God puts people in our lives. No, maybe funny isn't the word. Fascinating, perplexing, unexpected. Sometimes, it is the most interesting and surprising people who make the biggest impact. That describes Peter Grandich.

Shortly after meeting Peter, he came to my house for a Bible study and I realized that he was "different" than the other guys. First, Peter grew up in a house with a father who didn't go to church and a non-practicing Jewish mother, so he knew nothing about the scriptures. I mean nothing. If it wasn't in the movie The Ten Commandments, he didn't know about it—and he openly admitted that. "Charlton Heston didn't do it that way," he'd say, half joking. I thought, wow, this guy will be a challenge. And he was.

I soon learned Peter was also different in that he had an unusual gift for predicting financial market events, which resulted in his fifteen minutes of fame lasting a lot longer that just fifteen minutes.

Yet as different as he was, you will learn in *Confessions of a Wall Street Whiz Kid* that Peter was also just like so many of us who have battled anxiety, depression, panic attacks, and even thoughts of suicide or more. He's so different in some ways yet so alike in many others.

Though Peter's story is unique, it's common. It's real. We've all had our moments, our setbacks, our demons to contend with. Though we may not have suffered the crippling depression Peter did, we have all felt the sorrow of despair and the weight of fear that it brings.

In this funny, well written, entertaining, and very personal book, Peter tells how he twice rose to fame and fortune, but also how twice he nearly lost it all as he was crippled with depression and shame. He openly and honestly tells how his faith not only put him on the path to recovery, but literally saved his life.

Through Peter's experiences and open discussion of his life's events, we can all be encouraged that no matter how bleak life looks sometimes, with God's help and the help of your friends and community, you can live your days to their fullest.

Peter is one of those people who has a simple faith—and I mean that in the best possible way. It's not a theological faith or a heady faith. It's not a "you're supposed to forgive, so he does" or "you're supposed to show mercy, so he does." Like everything else in his life, Peter is an action guy who simply lives his faith in a plain and simple way. In all he does, he puts his love of God first and lets everything else fall in line behind that.

If more of us were like that, the world would be much better off. That's what Jesus talked to us about; living our faith, not just discussing it.

I hope you'll love this book as much as I do.

—Bill Wegner
Good News International Ministries
Howell, New Jersey

Confessions

of a

Former

Wall Street Whiz Kid

Fifth Edition

Chapter 1

An Unlikely Candidate

I believe every person is the direct result of the sum total of his or her life experiences. Where we have all been in our lives has a lot to do with where we are today and how we view the world.

I didn't grow up in an educated family; my parents didn't introduce me to Wall Street or investing at an early age; we didn't even have much money. In essence, I am probably the most unlikely person to someday be called "The Wall Street Whiz Kid."

~~~

I'm from New York. To anyone who has ever met me or heard me on TV or radio, that's a no brainer. I *sound* New York ... specifically, Bronx.

I was born in Manhattan in 1956, and, when I turned seven, my family moved north to one of New York's more family-oriented boroughs. My sister, who was eight years older, left home the following year to marry her childhood boyfriend. The couple moved to Brooklyn which, although it sounds close, is a long train or bus ride away, so for the next ten years I saw her only once or twice a year.

As a result, I basically grew up an only child. While my mother, Esther, worked constantly—mostly at secretarial jobs—my father spent much of my childhood unemployed. When he did work, it was often as a chauffeur for some big-named singers like Simon and Garfunkel and a sportscaster named Chris Schenkel. He'd occasionally find odd jobs doing other things, but was *not* working more than he *was* working.

The problem was: Dad was a gambler. Not to the point of loan sharks knocking on the door, but whatever money Dad managed to earn he gambled away at cards, the track, or the casinos. Gamblers, I have learned, are generally lazy people. That's why the thought of hitting it big on a bet is such a high for them. It's a way of beating the system and avoiding work. That describes my dad.

I guess it wasn't completely his fault. Like many of us, he had a dysfunctional upbringing and issues with his own family. As a matter of fact, by the time I was born he and his family were barely speaking. That rough Italian upbringing gave Dad a really bad temper, which got him fired more than once. I remember one job he lost because he punched a boss. People were often fearful of his temper. I know we were.

I used to tell people that my father was a police captain or he owned a private car service instead of admitting that Dad was a chauffeur or out of work. The reality was that I was embarrassed by my dad—by what he did, or more appropriately, what he didn't do. I was ashamed he didn't work hard and ashamed of the long stints when he didn't work at all. I later figured out that were it not for Mom's steady, modest income, we probably would have had an even more meager lifestyle. Thankfully, our simple apartment was in a rent-controlled building, which likely saved us more than once from living on the streets. Though my dad always managed to have a car to get around, Mom took only public transportation to and from work each day. There were no luxuries, no vacations. We had just enough clothes and food. I suppose living on the edge of lack is okay when your environment is a caring and nurturing one, but our lack extended to love. There was little money and less love. There was a lot of fear.

My father's name was Rudolph, but everyone called him Rudy. To the outside world, he was funny and generous. At home, the story was different. He verbally and physically abused me more times than I care to remember. I guess that was his way of taking out his frustrations, and he did it with books, chairs—whatever was handy and/or whatever he could throw. I remember we'd all wait until Dad woke up to see what kind of day it was going to be. If he was happy and smiling, we knew it would be a good day. If he got up and didn't talk, I'd run to my room to try to avoid the inevitable chaos and violence that could explode at any time.

My earliest memories of the physical abuse were around age eight or ten. I don't remember a whole lot, partly because it was such a crappy time and partly because it was a long time ago. But I do recall being hit by a toaster, wooden spoons, and other things. Sometimes it was just a punch to the face or a kick to the gut. Between the ages of thirteen and sixteen I ran away a few times, but there was no place to go. The longest I stayed away was seeking overnight refuge in the bowling alley. Eventually I had to go back home, and it was never pretty. I do recollect my mother sitting me down after

Dad's outbursts trying to somehow explain to me why he was like he was. Each time it ended with the fact that it wasn't my fault.

The last time he beat me I was twenty-one, and the argument was over me dating a thirty-five-year-old woman. Less than two years later, I'd leave for good.

In the last ten years of his life, he seemed to settle down physically and mentally. Maybe he mellowed. Maybe it was because he became estranged from some of his family members, so he became more focused on his own wife and kids. I don't know why, but he settled into a regular gig as a doorman—a position he seemed to enjoy. By this time, Mary and I were married, so I finally had real love in my life (the kind of love I never, ever had before), so over the years I came to forgive my dad for his decades of hurtful actions. It had been a long time since the violent days of my youth, and people who are raised in an abusive household are just happy when the hitting stops. I guess I never really trusted him again, just put up with him.

After Dad got the regular job as a doorman, he and Mom would travel to Atlantic City once a week, often stopping at my central New Jersey home to pick up my wife. On the way home from one such outing, he lingered in my living room. He'd had a good day at Trump's casino, saying that he beat "The Donald." (He liked the idea that if he won, it was coming right out of Donald Trump's pocket.) But that night he was uncharacteristically solemn, like he had something to share.

He sat me down in the living room and talked to me for perhaps the first time as a man and a father. As if seeking my forgiveness, he told me all the things he had done wrong. The abuse, the gambling, the lifestyle. He told me emphatically to never cheat on my wife, leading me to believe that he had succumbed to that evil. It was a sincere, heartfelt time we had … as if he was sharing with me what little wisdom he had in the hope that I wouldn't go down the same path he'd traveled. The whole exchange took maybe twenty minutes—about eighteen minutes longer than we'd ever spoken before.

Then he left, and I went about what I was doing. A few minutes later, he came running back up the stairs like he'd forgotten something, but he said he returned just to give me a kiss, which he hadn't done in years … or maybe never. Then, without a word, he ran back down the steps and he was gone.

The next morning he had a massive heart attack and died.

It was that day that I had my first real Christian experience: forgiveness. It's what our faith is based on. I knew I had forgiven my dad because when he died I wasn't mad at him … I felt sorry for him. After everything that had transpired between us, the lack of blame and culpability I felt had to have come from God. (That's where all real forgiveness comes from.) It wasn't something I could ever have done on my own, nor would I even have wanted to. But I did.

I didn't know it at that moment, but this was the first of many times where I saw the hand of God on my life.

~~~

As a boy, the one place Dad and I always found peace was at the racetrack. He was happy there. When I was seven or eight, he started taking me with him, and as a teenager, I got my first taste of gambling. From that point on, days were spent sneaking into Yonkers Raceway betting on horses, cards, bowling, and shooting pool for money at my home away from home, Fieldstone Bowling Alley.

There was never any real moral issue with gambling or hanging out in a pool hall since we were basically void of religion. My mother was a non-practicing Jew who was raised in an orphanage during the Depression, and my father a non-practicing Catholic. I was baptized as a baby, but my mother had thoughts of raising me Jewish. Dad, however, wouldn't have anything to do with it. Though I don't think he was a bigot, my father's immigrant Italian family was an anti-Semitic bunch and there was no way his kid was going to be a Jew. Remember, in 1947 when my parents got married, there weren't many "mixed" marriages like theirs.

So, I was left with zero religious training. Zilch. No church, no temple, no books, no nothing. No religion, period. We didn't believe there *wasn't* a God, we just didn't believe anything except what life had taught us. And life taught me a lot.

I did pretty well in school if you don't count being suspended three times in Junior High School 141. But, by the early seventies, racial tensions were high in the U.S., and likely nowhere higher than in New York City's public schools. When I was in the tenth grade at De Witt Clinton High School, I was robbed by a gang of African-American teens outside of school. It was nothing personal—I was just the wrong white guy in the wrong place at the wrong time. I resisted the attack, and fortunately a teacher saw the crime in progress and called the police. Later that night, two of the robbers were arrested. To retaliate for their buddies spending time at the local precinct, the next day a group of their friends attacked me in the hallway of school. The attack gave me a fierce prejudice that I wouldn't get over until many years later, and ultimately led to me not finishing the tenth grade. After a few months of summer school, I signed up to repeat the grade at a new school the following year.

A combination of boredom, an unfamiliar school, and other kids making fun of me caused me to quickly lose interest in schooling. At seventeen, I dropped out for good. With the exception of a few classes necessary for financial licensing, I have never returned to the halls of academia. I never got my high school equivalency diploma or GED, and have no college, trade school, or other formal education.

There have been times that I wish I had done things differently. I was never a great English student and I've always had to pay an editor or writer to correct my newsletters. That has cost me a small fortune. Some people, especially those who consider themselves in the "upper echelon," have been biased against me because I'm not a Wharton MBA with a cultured accent. Biff and Buffy generally don't rush to me with their business. But, the reality is that my streetwise ways have served me better than any piece of paper with an Ivy League name printed on it.

When I told my father I quit school he had only one piece of advice: "You better get a job." So, I took a job at a Korvette's department store for $2.93 an hour. When I wasn't flirting with the girls, I was selling hardware. Looking back, this is actually pretty ironic, since anybody who knows me knows that I have zero mechanical ability. Me, in the hardware department? Ha! That was 1973, and it was the first of many jobs that were taking me nowhere. But they kept me busy for a while until I found my next real passion: disco.

Depending on your age and where you are from, the thought of living for the discothèque either makes you laugh, gasp or cry. Nonetheless, I lived for Friday and Saturday nights and disco. Have you seen the movie *Saturday Night Fever*? No kidding, that was me. I wasn't exactly John Travolta, but I wasn't bad. The film and Travolta's Tony Manero character very accurately depicted the way my friends and I lived as part of the disco subculture that evolved around music, clothing, and dancing. Working a variety of dead-end jobs during the days just so we could make it to the disco at night. The leather jackets, wide shirt collar up over the jacket ... we epitomized the typical white-disco-guy persona.

We visited 2001 Space Odyssey (where *Saturday Night Fever* was filmed), Studio 54 and the other big discos in New York City. The Golden Hour in the Bronx was my home away from home and I spent many a night in Westchester County's Fudgies and The Milky Way. We valued our lives based on the amount of gold hanging around our necks and the cars we drove, and we judged the girls by the amount of makeup they wore and the volume of gum they could chew. Aah, to be young, naive, and without responsibility.

But the disco lifestyle was short lived. Though we had fun while it lasted, I soon found the bars and flings left me with a sense of emptiness. I guess the whole reason I got involved in that lifestyle was to try to make up for something lacking in my home life—searching for love and acceptance on the dance floor, in a bottle of booze and with countless women. It all ended in the spring of 1979 when I met my future wife, Mary Elizabeth Troy. A recent immigrant from Ireland who came for vacation and never left, Mary was a waitress at the Riverdale Diner in the Bronx. After meeting Mary, suddenly the partying and dancing and hedonistic lifestyle wasn't important to me. It was literally like a bell went off in my head, and was unlike anything I had ever felt before. I guess when you live without love for so long and then somebody loves you, the feeling of love is somehow amplified. It was remarkable.

Mary was different from any other woman I had ever met. To me, she was high class. That meant her thoughts weren't in the gutter like the other girls. She was extremely religious, a trait totally foreign to me, and she clearly came from a loving and nurturing family. In my eyes, she was gorgeous, and her heavy Irish brogue hooked me. When you added it all up, Mary had everything the other girls didn't. Despite the fact that for our first date I showed up in a t-shirt and took her to Pizza and Brew (not exactly a high-class joint), just eight weeks later, we were engaged to be married.

Soon after, my future father-in-law, Sean Troy, one of the finest human beings I have ever had the privilege to meet, arrived in the States to check me out and, per Irish tradition, I had to ask permission for his daughter's hand in marriage. What a concept, I thought. Getting your parents' permission? Outrageous. After having been with women who would do just about anything with anybody, I couldn't comprehend a woman who wouldn't marry without her father's blessing. So I knew I had to make the guy like me.

His whirlwind four-day trip came over the Thanksgiving holiday, flying in on Thursday and flying back out on Monday. He brought one of Mary's sisters with him for company, and the four of us spent the days socializing. Mary had told me her dad had raced greyhounds, so one day I took him to the track. By the end of the night he ended up winning, which made for a happy mood. Before leaving for the airport after their four-day visit, Mary and her sister retired to the bedroom giving me the high sign to make the "ask."

Those were the toughest words to ever come out of my

mouth, but I did it. Thankfully, he said yes, with his only request being that the wedding take place in Ireland. I said, "Sure, sure." Whatever it takes to marry Mary, I thought. The catch, I later learned, was that to be married in the Church of Ireland one must be Catholic. Needless to say, I became Catholic—not because of any spiritual yearning, but simply to get married. I would have become a Buddhist to marry her, it didn't matter to me. So, after eight or nine months of classes and a confession that took two hours (when you're doing your first confession at twenty-three it's a whole lot different than at eight), there I stood before the priest, surrounded by about five hundred eighth graders and three other adults, to receive my confirmation. Thus began my life as a Catholic.

Mary and I were married in a civil ceremony in New York in November, 1980, then in a church wedding in Ireland on April 20, 1981. (For five months we "lived in sin" in the eyes of the church because though legally married by a judge we had not been married in the church.) I returned home from Ireland with a new wife and a $25,000 dowry from my father-in-law. I was twenty-three and Mary was twenty-five.

In retrospect, I think my abusive father and desire for a stable, happy home likely accelerated our courtship. I saw Mary as a way out. Marriage sure beat my mother and father's house! So, our "happily ever after" began in an apartment in the Bronx, followed by a little duplex in suburban Andover, New Jersey, with Mary waitressing while I wound up in a job I really liked—and one that would drastically alter the course of my life—as a warehouse manager for Toshiba's copier division.

Chapter 2

Early Lessons Learned on "The Street"

While I was growing up, thanks to some "hot tips"—which were usually no more than lukewarm—my mother dabbled in stocks with what little extra money she had. My father, on the other hand, only bought stock once. He would often repeat the story, especially after I became a stockbroker, of how he bought into New York Airways in the 1960s. The company ran helicopters from the top of the Pan Am building to New York City's two airports. Two days after he bought the stock, before he even sent in the money, one of the company's helicopters was involved in a serious accident and several people died. Soon, the company was no more. That was Dad's lesson to me about investing in stocks and his last foray into the market.

Shortly after my wedding, I took a guided tour of Wall Street and the New York Stock Exchange and I was fascinated. The people, expensive suits, and palatial buildings were a foreign world to me. Everything about the process seemed fast-paced and exciting. It just reeked of wealth ... and I liked that.

Despite the fact that I had no stock market experience, there was something about Wall Street that called to me. I can't tell you what it was; the whole atmosphere seemed exhilarating to me.

As a result, I began making regular trips to the library to read up on investing, and was fortunate that a guy I worked with at the warehouse was heavily involved in the technical end of the market. We'd both read up on new investments and market trends, then we'd talk for hours and hours. He later introduced me to his broker, who patiently explained to me how the markets worked. In the process, I saw more of the nice cars the brokers drove, the clothing and jewelry they wore ... their lifestyle enticed me as much as the markets did. Growing up with next to nothing, you mistakenly believe, as I did, that people who had expensive things were somehow happier than us poor schmucks. They looked happy. I wanted that. I wanted all that "stuff" and that happiness for me. Not for my wife or future children, just for me. It was all about me.

So, in 1982, with nothing more than some self-study, a tourist's excursion, and some of the shared knowledge from my warehouse friend, I took $7,000 of Mary's dowry and began trading options. I bought, sold, bought, sold and as amazing as it sounds, in less than a year the account was worth about $100,000 minus taxes.

I thought we were set for life! Then I got my first hard Wall Street lesson. That's when a penny stockbroker (who shall remain nameless, but his firm was called Blinder Robinson but should have been called Rob-Them-Blind Robinson) convinced me to put all of the proceeds into a company called Telstar, which was going to put cable TV in hotels. One of the big draws was the fact that Ed McMahon was on the board of directors. Well, instead of "Heeeeeeeeeeere's Johnny," I heard, "Heeeeeeeeeeere's nothin'," as I lost the entire investment because the company went belly up. It happens to everyone at one time or another and is the basis for an old saying among financial professionals: If you want to end up with a million dollars in the stock market, start with two million.

Yet, the good (I think) that came out of this huge financial hit for a twenty-six-year-old suburban warehouse manager was this: Losing that much money made me passionate about becoming a stockbroker because I saw that even though I lost money, the broker still made money. It's a lesson I would never forget. Certainly I could do better than the guy who fleeced me, I thought. But I wasn't ready to jump right into being a broker since I still had to put food on the table and I knew brokers didn't make money right away; they had to build up a clientele. So I tested the investment waters a little further with my first real marketing angle: I started an investors club.

With one ad in a local north Jersey newspaper, thirty-seven people showed up for the first meeting of the New Jersey Investors Club. I conceived the idea of the club not to gain wisdom or knowledge, but as a way to meet potential clients. I had designs on becoming a broker, and since I didn't know the type of folks who had money to invest, starting the club gave me both credibility and a pool of prospective investors. We didn't combine our money and invest as a group as some clubs did, but instead pooled our ideas and shared speakers. It was my first real angle and within a short time, the club grew to nearly a hundred members. Naturally, I was the president.

We learned a lot from the professionals who spoke before the club. One such speaker was Bob Knapp, an honorable man who owned a small New York Stock Exchange-member firm. I point out the fact that Bob was moral and honorable because I soon found that he was not the norm. "Dishonorable" was, and often is, the status quo. Most brokers, I found, were simply interested in buying and selling stocks because with every trade they made a commission. Whether or not their clients were going to prosper was irrelevant. Bob was different. He seemed conscientious. Like me, he was analytical—he studied stocks and the market. He was smart. I liked him from the start. Bob talked about the markets and especially precious metals, and after the meeting was over he pulled me aside and complimented me on the great command I had over the group. When I talked, he said, people seemed to be riveted by what I was saying. "That's the type of stuff," he said, "you need to build a book of business." He said I'd be a great stockbroker.

Well, that's all it took. Less than half an hour of hearing Bob Knapp tell me I'd be successful and I was convinced. By the end of the night I decided to leave Toshiba and become a broker.

For the first time since dropping out of high school, I went "back to class" with a home study course for my Series 7 license. I read the book and took the sample tests over and over again until I was confident I would pass. But the broker idea didn't go over well at home; Mary was not thrilled. She felt I had a good job at Toshiba and shouldn't jeopardize it. It didn't help that my father-in-law in Ireland thought all stockbrokers were crooks, so he was against it, too. However, I persevered and eventually took the test in New York City and passed with flying colors.

In April 1984, I did something I never could have imagined a decade before: I became a stockbroker with Bob Knapp's firm. That's all it took—some cajoling and a few months of at-home training, and this high school dropout was now offering advice to business owners, executives, doctors, attorneys, and other professionals about how to invest their money.

A few weeks into my new career, I opened an account for a technology executive who did a fair amount of trading. That led to the first time (though not the last) I found myself in what I call "the gray area" where I was on neither the right nor the wrong side of the law ... let's just say I was straddling the line. You see, this guy bought lots of stock and options in a company called Decision Data, for which I believe he consulted. It didn't look that hot to me, so naturally I asked him why he was buying so much of the stock and options. He answered with a wink and a nod saying, "It's probably best if you don't know." Well, I didn't need a college education to figure out that this guy knew something I didn't. So, I bought it, too, and advised the clients I had to do the same. It was no surprise when the company received a takeover offer and the stock price jumped. I didn't ask any questions, but profited nicely—both personally and professionally.

After the transaction was complete, I remember thinking that I had just made more money on that one trade than I had ever made in an entire year. I subsequently took up the mantra, "It's not *who* you know, but **what** *they* know."

~~~

Though some of the people from the investors club became clients, I needed to build my business bigger. However, the traditional way brokers find clients, cold calling, gave me sweaty palms. I hated it, and I wasn't very good at it. I was so depressed after the very first hang-up that I knew I had to find another way to attract clients. That's when Bob

Knapp suggested I write a newsletter. The idea was for me to document my views and forecasts, and use the publication as a tool to drum up business. The concept was approved by the compliance guy in the office, and in just one day the newsletter was born. I wrote, typed, made two hundred copies and sent out the first edition of *The Grandich Letter*.

I sent it to friends and clients, I put an ad in the paper for a "free investment newsletter," and gave them out at Rotary Club meetings. I can even remember putting them on car windshields in the parking lot. I was willing to try anything at that point. I was desperate for clients.

The newsletter resulted in only a little bit of new business, but what it did was start my love affair with putting my ideas in writing. Since that first edition in 1984, I have written millions of words in newsletters, newspapers, magazines, books, and my blog.

~~~

One day, much to my surprise, Bob Knapp announced that he had to sell the firm because of financial troubles. Soon after, he left and joined a firm called Underhill Associates. My clients and I went with him. It was run by, in my opinion, the first really bad man I came to meet in the business. Soon, I began to question my decision. The joke in the office was the firm should be called "Underwater Associates" because all our stocks ended up "under water." We also called the place "the home of *submerging* growth stocks" because they all tanked.

But it was at Underhill that I saw for the first time how one lucky break in the media can make millions. One of the Underhill deals was with Mel Fisher, the renowned treasure hunter. One morning shortly after Bob and I arrived, ABC News broke the story that Fisher's crew had just found the mother lode from the sunken Spanish galleon *Nuestra Señora de Atocha* off Key West, Florida. As a result, the phones rang off the hook for a week or so and we were swamped. I'll bet a couple of guys made $50,000 that week selling limited partnerships with Mr. Fisher. They did more business in a week than I could do in a year. It amazed me. Though the publicity was short-lived, it opened my eyes to the power of the media and what it could do for my bottom line. It's a lesson I never forgot.

One other good thing came out of my short stay at Underhill: the company paid for my newsletter to be professionally produced. My slick newsletter caught the eye of an executive at Philips, Appel and Walden (PAW), members of the New York Stock Exchange, and he invited me to his office. I went, I liked him right away, and it seemed like no sooner than I started at Underhill I was gone, and this time Bob Knapp followed me.

~~~

My new boss at PAW was Bob Trause, the branch manager. He was a great guy with a fast-paced, high-energy manner fueled by what seemed like gallons of coffee. One day we counted twenty-three cups—that's right, twenty-three cups of high-test, caffeinated, burn-a-hole-in-your-gut coffee. By the end of each day he was either blissfully happy or totally disenchanted with life.

When you think of a NYSE-member firm back then, companies like Merrill Lynch, Dean Witter and Prudential usually come to mind—old, prestigious firms dealing in bonds, retirement accounts and blue chip stocks like IBM.

Over-the-counter (OTC) firms, on the other hand, usually handled the cheap "penny" stocks. Well, PAW was a penny stock house dressed up as a NYSE firm. Though they were a member of the NYSE to try to give the impression of prestige, their primary business was selling initial public offerings (IPOs) in the $1–$5 range, not the big stock deals most people would assume.

Most of the brokers, including me, were stock jocks, salespeople who worked the phones to try to sell financial products. Financial planning was not yet the way of the world, so most brokers earned their money trading stocks. There were a cast of characters in this office that rivaled any soap opera, but two always had my eye. There was Ray. He was a nut job, plain and simple. Sometimes we'd find him crouched underneath his desk talking to his clients in a whisper. Other times he would be loud and boisterous with arms flailing. He fit the stereotype of the high-pressure penny stock broker and could say just the right thing to influence or even shame the customer into making a purchase.

"If I was selling you gold for twenty dollars an ounce you'd find the money..." and

"Who wears the pants in your family, you or your wife?"

But the best one I remember was when he was obviously not getting the prospect to buy and I heard him say, "Do you have $300?"

I knew we didn't take orders that small.

Obviously, the prospect asked if he wanted him to buy just $300 worth of the stock, because I then heard Ray say, "No, I want you to buy a gun because you'll want to shoot yourself when you see what this stock does and you're not in it."

This guy was priceless. And he made money. He was always one of the top five producers in the office.

There were other characters. One of the PAW brokers did nothing but limited partnerships (LPs). Back then, they were sold as tax shelters and you could invest a dollar and claim losses of two, three, or four. The law has since been changed and they are no longer the tax shelters they were, but at the time LPs were most often used by investors for write-offs. This particular broker especially pushed LPs when the underwriter offered incentive vacations in return for a specific sales volume. We later learned that he would take girlfriends on these trips and tell his wife he was doing "due diligence" on a potential partnership. One day, after his wife obviously found out about one of his affairs, she showed up in the office and poured hot coffee all over him. Two days later he was back in the office hawking the LPs. And that was just another day in the dysfunctional life at PAW. The assumption by the public was that the majority of people working within the firm were highly educated, clean-cut, all-around good people. When, in fact, it was a bunch of misfits, gambling junkies, and a cast of unsavory characters dressed up as brokers.

~~~

When pushing IPOs, every single deal required a due diligence meeting where brokerage firms underwriting and/or selling the deal would meet to hear about the deal. PAW did mostly all their own deals so it ended up just PAW brokers at most of the meetings. We learned to judge the potential of the company and its stock by the spread of food that was put out at the meeting. Inevitably, the more they tried to schmooze us, the less they had to offer. If a superb meal was given with gifts, we concluded the stock was a dud. If the spread consisted of cheese and crackers, we surmised the stock had potential. It's uncanny how accurate our grading system was.

One such deal was a company called New York City Shoes. The sizzle was supposed to be the fact that every pair of shoes sold for ten dollars. When we arrived at the hotel for the due diligence meeting, the entire banquet room was set up as a New York City Shoes store. The dinner was top-notch, and we each received numerous pairs of shoes as gifts. From this glitzy show, we figured the deal was tough even before looking at the prospectus.

I had learned early on that the key to any IPO was getting past two factors in the prospectus: dilution and legal actions. How much money did they have, how were they going to spend it, and did they have any legal issues? In the New York City Shoes case, dilution was almost 100 percent. The majority of the money was going to pay off debt (much of it owed to officers of the company) and back taxes, which appeared in the legal action page. The company had not paid state taxes, citing the need for capital to grow the firm. As a result of this information, I passed on the deal because I didn't think the company would amount to much. Others didn't, however—to them it was another sale and another commission. They weren't particularly concerned whether their clients were going to make money, only whether or not *they* were making money. In less than a year of going public, the company went bankrupt, but not before a lot of stockbrokers made money.

Yet another deal we did was called Steve's Ice Cream. At their meeting we were served no dinner, given no gifts and only got a single pint of ice cream. That stock tripled in the first year and getting much of the IPO was impossible because it was in such high demand.

One company I was involved in was a generic drug maker called Zenith Labs. Zenith was working on a drug that, if approved, could potentially drive the stock price considerably higher. At their annual meeting, the CEO announced the drug's approval and said the approval information had just been announced to the world in a press release. I rushed to the phone booth—there were no cell phones or BlackBerrys back then—and called the office. For some unknown reason, the news of the drug's approval had not yet hit the wires, so the stock's price was largely unchanged. We bought call options and shares and later that day the news hit and the stock rose nicely. Ka-ching.

Along the way, I also learned the value of trusting my instincts. Along the east coast, the electronics store Crazy Eddie, owned by Brooklyn, New York-based ERS Electronics, was well-known for its low prices and loud spokesperson, "Eddie," who was named for the store's co-founder Eddie Antar. We began to make a market in the stock under four dollars and the commission, also known as the "chop," was sometimes 3/8 of a point. That was nearly 10 percent, which meant you could sell just a thousand shares and earn $387. Nothing makes a stock more interesting to a broker than the chop. Takeover rumors began to circulate, so I began to buy heavily, no matter what the commission was. I ended up with the biggest position in a stock for clients in my short career. Soon after, a company called Entertainment Management, which traded on the Amex, made a bid at eight dollars for Crazy Eddie. The stock went above eight dollars, suggesting the market believed a higher bid would be needed.

I was surprised to learn that PAW was working for

Entertainment Management, and I was asked to join some of our officers at a Crazy Eddie warehouse. While there, we started discovering that some of the boxes were empty, even though TVs and other electronics were supposed to be in them. It seemed not to faze some other brokers, but I took this as a bad sign and called all my clients to sell around eight dollars. Brokers in my office laughed at me because the stock was expected to go to a ten-dollar or even twelve-dollar offer, but to me something just didn't smell right. The stock did, in fact, rise to around nine dollars a share; however, within a short period, it was discovered that the brothers who owned Crazy Eddie cooked the books and the stock fell hard. My clients were already out, and so was I. Me seeing a few empty boxes may have been construed as insider information, but who's to say that because a couple of boxes were empty that the owners were crooks? Was this legal? It was gray ... deep gray!

Incidentally, in 1989, Crazy Eddie declared bankruptcy and was liquidated. Antar, who was nicknamed "The Darth Vader of Capitalism" by U.S. Attorney Michael Chertoff, was eventually charged with a series of crimes and did a few years in "Club Fed" for fraud. He was ordered to pay more than $150 million in fines and a billion (yes, billion with a "b") dollars in judgments to defrauded stockholders, whom I doubt will ever see a dime.

Chapter 3

The Media Crowns the "Kid"

During my short tenure at Underhill, I saw firsthand how powerful the media was as a business-building tool. I figured if I could harness that power I could really build my book of business, while at the same time building my status, reputation, and growing ego.

I had a friend who was a reporter for a little weekly newspaper in central New Jersey, and after I got a promotion in 1987, I convinced him to do an article about me, telling my story as a high school dropout who bucked the odds to become a Wall Street stockbroker. The feature was really good, and I made copies and sent it around to a few other papers. Using that article as bait, along with copies of *The Grandich Letter*, I was able to hook the business editor of one of New Jersey's largest dailies to do a story. Then, I repackaged both articles and sent them to some even bigger fish.

As a result, I got myself booked on Eva Dorn's show on the Financial News Network—FNN, which was later bought out by CNBC. Appearing on the show meant a grueling day-long flight to Los Angeles, the half-hour 4:30 p.m. appearance, and immediately off to the airport to catch the redeye back to Newark. Though tiring, it was worth it when the phones started ringing off the hook. That first appearance generated hundreds of requests for a free copy of my newsletter. Thankfully, Eva liked me as a guest, and I was invited back. A month later I flew out again, after which we received even more responses. Within a few weeks of my first appearance, I had several dozen new clients, and every time I appeared, the phones in the office rang like mad—so many calls, in fact, that I had to give the leads to other guys in the office. It was remarkable.

To my great pleasure, I found that the media is kind of like a virus: It spreads. One media success leads to another and another. I started getting interviewed regularly on TV and radio, and every time I appeared I ended up with a few new clients. Things were great.

It was about that time that PAW's head of investment strategy left the firm, and Bob and I went to talk to the boss about me filling his shoes. The boss knew I was responsible for bringing in a great deal of new business thanks to my growing media profile. With little more than a conference call and a follow-up meeting, I was made vice president of investment strategy.

For me and my ego, it was too good to be true! It didn't mean any more money, but what a great title, I thought. Keep in mind that I had been in the business a grand total of three years at that point. I was a young, inexperienced high school dropout entrusted with the strategic direction of thousands of company clients.

That was perhaps the first time that the status of my work

became important to me. I remember how excited I was as I told Mary about the new job and all the money I could make. Of course, Mary was unimpressed, as those trappings never mattered to her, but she trusted me. As a matter of fact, she always trusted. She never questioned. A devout Catholic who truly practiced her faith, Mary had always believed that God would take care of everything. Even if I screwed things up, she knew she could depend on God.

~~~

In August of 1987, in the midst of all the media attention I was drawing, things in the market made me very uneasy. Based on my "long-standing" history of three whole years in the business, I believed that the market was set up for a big crash. The thing about that was it was pure instinct. A sophisticated guess. Following my gut. There was no technical analyzing that went into it, no fundamental examination. Just Peter thinking, hmmm, something doesn't feel right here. Bear in mind that I didn't have the experience or the intelligence to have concluded this. But I did. So, I advised all of my clients to sell. Everything. Get out of the market. In hindsight, I now know this was the second time I felt the hand of God in my life. It was He who gave me that insight because I sure as heck couldn't have come up with that on my own.

Note that I told them the market "will" crash. Not that it "might," "could," or "should." In this business you never use unconditional words like it "will." You always cover your butt with a long legal disclaimer or you dance around the facts with less precise phrases like "the markets show weakness and may dip" or "the market is poised to fall sharply."

But I used the word "will."

After issuing my forecast I was called up to the boss's office post haste and given two options: either retract my forecast or resign.

I was interested in neither. When I asked why, his explanation was succinct and very matter-of-fact. He explained that, "Ninety percent of all people will never sell *everything*. Though they might sell *some* holdings they'll hang on to a few that are their favorites for some reason or another."

"If you're wrong, they'll never listen to you again. And if you're right and this terrible thing happens, they aren't going to be able to profit from you because they've already lost a lot of money," he explained. "Look at the 10 percent who do listen to you: half will be too afraid to step back in when you tell them to, so the net effect is that only 5 percent will profit from this advice."

Then he said something I have never forgotten, "On Wall Street, no firm can survive with only 5 percent of its clients profiting."

From a strictly sales point of view, I guess he was right. But I never looked at it that way. I just assumed that you should do the right thing and tell people the way you see it. He thought more about the bottom line.

I didn't retract my statement. I didn't resign. And, somehow, I didn't get fired. I stuck to my prediction.

It's important to note here that what truly separated me from the pack of prognosticators on Wall Street was not necessarily that I said there was going to be a crash. There were a few other people who waved the caution flag, though I don't remember anyone else saying it with such conviction.

What made my call different was the fact that my employer was demanding a retraction, and I wouldn't budge. That was a very unpopular move on my part.

On August 25, just eleven days after my doomsday prediction, the Dow Jones Industrial Average (DJIA) had risen seventy-five points, which was a big move at that time. I became the laughingstock of the firm. Other brokers would call to tell me that Kmart was hiring and I should go apply, or they just left voicemails asking what I was going to do for my next career.

PAW had several office locations, and one day I got an interoffice delivery—a package that stank to high heaven. It was a box full of "doggie doo" and a note saying "This is what I think of your forecast." Naturally, the note was unsigned and we never figured out which of my supportive colleagues sent it. I always wondered how the poor messenger put up with driving a box of dog poop from office to office.

I just put up with it and stuck to my guns.

In mid-September, to the surprise of most on Wall Street, the markets started to show signs of faltering. Then, on October 19, 1987, "Black Monday" hit and the DJIA dropped 508 points to 1739. It was the largest one-day decline in recorded stock market history at the time.

If you weren't in the market back then or are too young to recall, you may not realize the severity of this crash. This was big. Huge. It was being compared to the crash in the 1920s when brokers literally took their own lives by jumping out of windows. The fear was the economy would sink and unemployment would become severe.

On October 20, the day after the colossal beating on Wall

Street, I put out what became my second "famous" prediction: I stated that the market would be at a new all-time high within two years. Nobody could picture it. The devastation was too colossal. They all thought I was nuts. In the depths of the despair and depression and recession on Wall Street, they just couldn't imagine that we'd rebound in less than twenty-four months. Remember, the 1920s crash sparked the Great Depression and years of financial and human suffering in the U.S.

But, hard as it was to imagine, out of the doom of that Black Monday crash the markets went to incredible heights within the next two years, proving my call spot on. Thus, my second famous prediction. Note that there was no way I was "qualified" to make this call, either. That's how I know it was God. At my level of ability and knowledge dumb luck would allow me to get one of those predictions correct. But to get both of them right? Yup, it was God. Had I not made those two calls I would never have the notoriety I have today.

A reporter named Steve Crowley who did business reporting on ABC's nationally televised morning show *Good Morning America* picked up on my forecasts and ended up doing a segment on me. Because of my foresight, my youth—I was just thirty-one years old when most investment strategists on the Street were gray-haired old men—and the fact that my only "education" was the school of hard knocks, he dubbed me "The Wall Street Whiz Kid"—a nickname that has followed me, for better or for worse, ever since.

Needless to say, that interview and the resulting publicity really escalated my career, resulting in more media appearances, more clients, and more money. I couldn't have been happier. And, of course, the media buzz continued to spread like a virus in a room full of runny-nosed preschoolers.

About a year later I was asked to appear on what was then the hottest and most highly charged TV show at the time, *The Morton Downey, Jr. Show.*

This was long before the days of Jerry Springer or sensational, reality TV shows. Morton was a right-wing chain smoker who lit up the airwaves in more ways than one. Things got so out of hand on his set that guests and audience members had to go through metal detectors at the front door. Though metal detectors may be the norm now, in the 1980s they were an anomaly. At first, I refused to appear on his show fearing I would be the target of Downey's on-air rage. It was no secret that he absolutely hated Wall Street types, yuppies, and anyone who drove a BMW. But the producers assured me I would be the hero and the other Wall Street guests would be Morton's target. They said he really wanted to tell the story about a regular guy who never finished high school yet warned of the crash months before it happened and was largely ignored.

I finally agreed to go, and as it turned out I was, indeed, made to look like a champ for calling the crash. The other guy who showed up (they invited dozens and only one guy had the guts to come on air), Louis Ehrenkrantz, was verbally attacked. Downey chewed him up and spit him out on national TV. It was a slaughter. To his credit, Ehrenkrantz did a superb job of defending Wall Street, and we later became good friends. Lou passed away a few years later and I miss him.

After the broadcast, Downey brought me backstage to his dressing room, thanked me, told me how much he liked having me as a guest, and we, too, became friends. A year or so later, he moved to CNBC and I appeared on his new show there.

Life couldn't be better.

~~~

As a result of calling the crash and all the media attention, I got what would be the first of many invitations to speak before a big, live audience; the Sound Money Investors (SMI) conferences, which were held offshore and in the U.S.

SMI was run by a controversial, eccentric American guy name Bob White who wore overalls and sandals at the shows. He was the author of the *Duck Book*, an *über*-conservative book best paraphrased as: "The U.S. of A. is going to hell in a handbasket, the commies are taking over, and we're losing our market share. God help America." He was so unconventional that his publishing company and SMI were both kicked off the Vancouver Stock Exchange, which was nearly impossible back then on Vancouver's highly controversial exchange.

The very first time I spoke at SMI was in Orlando, Florida, and I will never forget it. It was an auditorium full of right-wing, flag-waving, wealthy investors—mostly white men aged sixty years and older and clearly highly conservative in their political views. I always found it an interesting paradox that while they wrapped themselves in the American flag, the most popular speaker at the conference was always the guy who taught them how to move their money offshore and avoid paying taxes.

During my presentation, I shared my thoughts that the DJIA would recover to new highs and how I felt gold would go lower. I was heckled and booed like a New York Giants fan at a Philadelphia Eagles game! This was a hard-core, hard-asset crowd, and I was telling them things they didn't want to hear. One man actually rose and screamed for me to get off the stage and proceeded to tell me why the stock market crash in '87 would just be the beginning of a long decline. He ranted about why gold was going up, how the Soviet Union was going to eventually take over the U.S., and how his gold would allow him to bribe his way to Canada.

He was typical of the investors there.

"What makes you think the Russians won't overthrow Canada?" I asked him.

I was ready to walk off and go home when suddenly a well-dressed younger man came on stage, grabbed the microphone and began to lambaste the audience for the way they treated me. He went on to tell them about how right I had been in the past and encouraged me to not only finish, but to come back to the next show. I don't know if it was because he believed in what I was saying or just didn't want one of the guests to be mistreated, but after he spoke the audience calmed a bit, even though they thought I was dead wrong. I later learned he was Chuck Arnold, and he worked with Bob White selling franchises and other business opportunities.

So, I become a regular at SMI shows and met many new clients in my travels with them.

Months later, while Chuck Arnold and Bob White were in Belize looking at investment condos, Bob was shot and killed. The story was a murky one. It seems that while they were on the beach looking at the properties, an assailant with a machete supposedly came out of the jungle. A struggle ensued and the assailant allegedly shot Bob to death with Bob's own gun. Other details were sketchy.

Not long after, Chuck took control of SMI with a man I will

call just "Doc." Remember Boss Hogg from the eighties TV show *The Dukes of Hazzard*? That was Doc. He was always making a hard sell of whatever crazy product or scheme SMI was peddling.

After a while, many of the speakers, including me, received a fax from Doc claiming that Chuck had had Bob killed, and he had proof. A few days later, Doc was found dead in what was ruled a suicide. Needless to say, this cast a real shadow on Chuck and SMI. Though the conferences continued for a while, soon Chuck got involved in touting stocks for big money. The media began to question his validity, regulators either charged him or threatened to, and he disappeared into the night.

And so did my involvement with SMI. By that time, I and many of the other legitimate speakers didn't want anything to do with this guy.

~~~

Like many investment firms, PAW was mortally wounded in the crash, so I looked for greener pastures. By 1989, I was with a firm I could literally walk to from my home, AFM Investments. It was small—three partners, two of whom I liked very much. One of them, Martin Saltzman, was and still is the most honest stockbroker I have ever met. Other brokers would engage in practices like giving a client a quote of the high price of the day instead of where a stock was trading at the time. Marty was incapable of any of that.

It was at that small, unassuming firm that I really solidified my "legend in my own mind" status. I was hot stuff—or at least I told myself that every day. I took the Ten Commandments and turned them into the "Ten Suggestions" and picked and chose which ones to follow or ignore. My faith consisted of going to church every now and then mostly for show, while my wife went weekly as a true profession of her unwavering faith.

My business was growing rapidly and my narcissistic attitude was producing regular appearances at conferences, a cable television program, an expanding newsletter subscriber list, and numerous national TV and radio interviews. *The Grandich Letter* spawned The Grandich Hotline, a recorded message I updated each week for subscribers who called in to listen. I also started several more newsletters including *The Blue Chip & Income Report*, *The High Flyer Report*, and *North of the Border*. I didn't need God. I was a god—an investment god.

I began several years of regular appearances on CNBC, after an airplane trip I spent sitting next to Neal Cavuto, the current Fox News business editor who was working for CNBC at the time. One show I will never forget put me right smack in that gray area again, thanks to noted financial reporter Dan Dorfman. Dorfman gained notoriety by making a daily commentary on stocks. He became so popular that if he gave a favorable report on CNBC, the stock would fly. If he panned it, the stock would swoon. This particular time I was at CNBC studios before my interview and for some reason they had me sitting in the control room instead of the green room, which was the norm. On one of the monitors in the control room, a tech had posted the stock information Dan Dorfman was going to speak about later that afternoon, and I could see it was clearly a bullish report. Dorfman was to come on 45 minutes after my segment.

Needless to say, as soon as my interview was over I raced to a phone and told my colleagues what was to come. We all bought shares, the stock popped and then we all sold. Yes, we profited tidily. Was this illegal? Good question. There was no assurance that what I saw on the monitor was accurate, and even less assurance that what he had to say would lead to the stock rising. However, you and I both know it was morally wrong. But morally wrong is no show stopper on Wall Street. It's an everyday occurrence.

The CNBC-TV appearances also led to me meeting two very popular CNBC hosts and experts in the world of finance, Ken and Daria Dolan. I became a regular on their program and we became close personal friends. My ego, however, was really starting to get in the way of rational judgment. I was such a legend in my own mind and always looking for an angle to boost "me" that I named Daria Dolan as my daughter's godmother. Bringing the Dolans into the family tree seemed like a great business move at the time, but I later learned that it hurt my sister deeply. It took years for our relationship to recover.

Around 1990, I became friends with a newsletter writer named Glenn Cutler who wrote *Market Mania*. Glenn also had a very popular daily fax service. The partners at AFM, who had all come from a notorious penny stock house before forming the current company, became aware of a stock that happened to do business down the road from us—one that their former penny-stock house was promoting big-time. The stock had risen from pennies to a few dollars a share. We alerted Cutler to the fact that their projections were way off and there was no possible way they could meet those numbers, and he consequently panned it in the section of his fax service called "Skull and Crossbones." The stock started to drop hard. I tipped off the local newspaper business editor, the writer who had profiled me a few years earlier leading to my first FNN appearance, who picked up on the story and the share price really began to tank. (My tip was a sort of currency I used to further my career: I gave him a little technical info he otherwise would not have known, and in return I scored points with him. He quoted me more, I got a stronger reputation, attracted more clients and made more money.) Soon after, the principal showed up at our office, claiming he was losing millions and believed we were to blame. He was so angry that for a while we checked under the hood before starting the car to be sure no explosives had been planted. We really didn't know what he would do. Eventually nothing happened and the stock fell to just six cents.

Another visit to the gray area was through a stock called Itex. My associates and I had been big buyers. The company CEO had told me he was discussing doing a "toxic" financing, where the buyer of the financing received more shares if the stock price kept going lower. We saw the house that was set to do the financing always being the lowest offer. We assumed they were shorting the stock. Unsolicited, the CEO rang me one morning in a huff saying he was going to cancel the potential financing with these "toxic" folks. Faster than a speeding bullet, yours truly and associates were buying all the shares we could. The toxic boys just kept selling to us despite our continuous buying for about two hours. Then suddenly but not surprisingly, they left the offer. The share price began to move up and they became big buyers. The stock rose at least 25 percent, and we sold our shares for a small fortune. Gray? Absolutely. Darker? Perhaps.

~~~

New clients were an almost everyday occurrence thanks to all the media and TV coverage I was receiving. God played almost no role as far as I was concerned. It was my brilliant mind that did it all. Me, me, me. I was the self-proclaimed chairman and CEO of the Me, Myself and I society.

I had a lot of great clients, some who became lifelong friends. One, who contacted me after reading about me in *Barron's*, wanted to know what my minimum account was to trade options. I told him $5,000.

"I would think someone of your caliber would have a much higher minimum," he said, surprised.

"I do," I replied.

I explained that normally my minimum was $100,000, but what I wanted him to do was write the $5,000 check out directly to me and I would save him $95,000 by *not* letting him trade options. Options are a broker's delight but can be financial suicide for the general public who try to trade them. He obviously appreciated my candor and turned out to be a good client and friend. Later he became a shareholder in my company.

I also had some really bad clients. One came to our office with a portfolio of highly speculative gold stocks and penny stocks and opened three accounts. We did lots of trading per his instructions, including options. In one of the accounts, he had us buy calls in Eastman Kodak. We were down about $30,000 when he suddenly said he never wanted to own them. No doubt about it, he was outright lying. We told him to hang on, that the stock would bounce back, but he sold. The option would have turned out to be profitable in two weeks if he had held.

A couple of weeks later he transferred his accounts out of the office and a few months later we got notice that he filed an arbitration case against us claiming unauthorized trading on the EK trade. He lost about $30,000 and was seeking to cover his losses. His only real "evidence" was the fact that he didn't sign the option papers for one of the accounts. He had filled out the forms for all three accounts in his own handwriting and either forgot to or purposely did not sign one of the three forms. Because it was unsigned, he tried to claim that he wasn't aware of the risk involved.

In the brokerage business, you're assumed guilty until proven innocent. You're also hit with lots of so-called "hindsight analogies." Sure, if a stock went from ten dollars to one dollar it's not a good thing. But what were the circumstances when it was ten dollars? Was proper due diligence done? Were rules followed? Brokers shouldn't be "guilty" just because a stock doesn't work. Heck, if people were always held accountable for being wrong, weathermen would be sued all the time. What happens in most arbitration cases happened to us: as the hearing came close, the parties agreed to settle. We ended up paying $3,500 and did so only because, as our lawyer put it, "It's the cost of doing business." Besides, we'd end up paying either way since that would be his fee for a day in court.

~~~

These stories—these clients—were my formal education. And I've learned more from them than I ever could have learned in a classroom. I wouldn't trade that teaching for anything. But the more I learned it seemed the more I lacked the basic components for a truly successful life—humility, faith, and a real relationship with God. But he was still working on me, and so was Mary.

Chapter 4

The Rise

In 1991, we learned Mary was pregnant. Since we had been led to believe that she might never be able to have children, we were elated. Well, at least Mary was. Though I was thrilled with the idea that she *could* get pregnant, I can't say that I was thrilled with the fact that she *was* pregnant. Like many other would-be parents, I didn't think I was ready to have a child. In spite of my growing income, I wondered if we could afford it. I also didn't know if a child would get in the way of *my* plans—*my* career, *my* business, *my* ego. And my single biggest fear was that I would end up parenting like my father, and that my child would fear and loathe me. I was panicked.

At the time she became pregnant, we lived in a small house in suburban New Jersey a few blocks down the street from AFM where I worked. Mary had continued to work, but immediately stopped once we found out the news.

Then, our expectation turned to fear. Mary suddenly had high blood counts. An ultrasound wasn't conclusive but suggested spina bifida, a birth defect in which the baby's backbone and spinal canal do not close before birth. Our doctors wanted Mary to undergo an amniocentesis to check for possible birth defects. She refused the risky test, saying that it didn't matter what kind of abnormality or deformity the baby may have; she was having this child either way. That night, on the way home from the doctor's office, she said she wanted to go to a "healing service" with Father Brendan Williams, a dynamic Irish priest at St. Veronica's Roman Catholic Church in Howell, New Jersey. Ironically, I walked past that church every time I walked to the office, but rarely ventured inside for Mass. But on this night, I went. I would have done anything. I was desperate for something—medical or miracle—to heal our unborn child.

The service was a typical Mass, after which people lined up to receive prayer from the priest and lay people. Being one of the few men in attendance, I was asked to be a "catcher." At healing Masses, the people who are being prayed for often get so emotional and filled with the Holy Spirit that they collapse or faint. We call it being "slain in the Spirit." The "catcher" is the person who catches them as they fall, ensuring a safe, soft landing on the floor or nearby chair.

As I stood behind the people Father was praying for, I heard them seeking help for some really awful problems—broken families, homelessness, deadly diseases—problems that seemed far, far worse than mine. It was humbling. Even though there were three other prayer teams, Mary ended up in my line with Father Williams. So, I stood behind my faithful wife as she received prayer in a brogue as thick as hers. He prayed that the Lord would heal our baby. He prayed for Mary's health. He prayed for me. Then, from his heavy accent came unrecognizable syllables—babble, which I later learned was speaking in tongues, and I watched in awe as Mary collapsed back into my arms. I was shocked.

Now, you have to know Mary to appreciate this, but trust me when I tell you that she wouldn't faint just because everyone else was passing out. She's a no-nonsense kind of woman. But she went down like a rock. At first, I was alarmed. She's my wife; I can tell when she's "sleeping," and she was out like a light. Father immediately leaned over to me and said in his Irish brogue, "The Holy Spirit is here but for what reason I don't know."

This whole situation was very surreal to me. I didn't quite know what to think of the experience, but it moved me.

Mary awoke less than a minute later and I told her what Father had said. She was gleaming with hope. She told me she immediately felt healed. Certainly, I didn't know what she meant and I didn't have any of these same feelings, but it gave her peace, so who was I to second-guess. It was a remarkable, Godly experience that neither of us will ever forget, and would eventually end up bringing me much closer to both God and Mary.

From that night on, Mary had no worries. Faithful servant that she is, she knew that although the doctors may have been right, that God had healed our child and the hole in the spine no longer existed. In Mary's eyes, our baby was healthy. Yet, I still worried.

A few months later, however, my fears were allayed when Mary gave birth to a perfect and beautiful baby girl we named Tara. With the exception of a hammer toe, Tara was the picture of health. Watching the birth of my daughter was and will remain the most amazing and thrilling moment of my existence. That sweet baby girl would become the love of my life.

That night, as I went down in the elevator, for the very first time I felt a real connection to God. I prayed hard and asked Him to help me be a better father than my dad had been, and for the first time, I really felt He was listening.

~~~

Though some of fatherhood came naturally to me, some of it was very foreign. I loved and adored and played with her whenever I could, but I was nearly unable to care for Tara. I can't explain it, but I just couldn't change a diaper. One thing God never gave me was a strong stomach. At the mere thought of a stinky diaper I gagged, coughed, and hollered for Mary. With the possible except of one or two, Mary changed every single diaper. The Wall Street Whiz Kid flunked Diapering 101.

God blessed us with a very happy, blissful baby. Like many sleep-deprived new parents, we were walking zombies for a while. However, we eventually figured that part out and things in the Grandich home were great ... just as I had planned. Recently, my now-grown daughter told me she has never feared me, and never thought I took my frustrations out on her, so I guess He really was listening that day in the elevator.

~~~

Prior to Tara's birth, we moved to our first house of our own. Our previous place was too small for a family and raising Tara there would have been difficult at best. So, Mary and I decided that she would stay at home with Tara in our new, modest home. Little did we know that my career was about to take a bad turn.

The partners at AFM Investments decided they no longer wanted to handle stock trading and they were shifting to a financial planning business model. Since I didn't feel qualified to become a financial planner (the only thing I knew how to do at that point was buy and sell stocks), they asked me to leave. I was very hurt and angry. How could they do this after all we had been through together, not to mention the fact that I was a brand-new father?

While I quickly found a home at a nearby firm after leaving AFM, I soon saw the all-too-familiar signs that something wasn't right. One of the partners was a strange character named Hank. He was always whispering to clients, but when one client in particular called, he closed his door in secrecy. He had instructed us that no one else may ever talk to her. My suspicions were correct and Hank was ultimately found guilty of embezzling from this lady and others, and he was sentenced to seven years in prison.

There was only so much of that I could take. I wanted to serve my clients with no dishonesty and no "gray areas" and without the risk of building a book of business and then being fired. I decided to open my own firm. There was just one obstacle: I didn't have the funds to do so.

I had seven clients who actively traded the market. I approached them and proposed that each would put up a sum of money for an interest in the new firm and, in return, I would reduce their commissions to the point where they would recoup their investment over time. They all agreed, and The Peter Grandich Company was born. Since I didn't have all the necessary licenses to trade on my own, I contacted Bob Knapp, who came to work with me in my grand new office on Route 34 in Wall Township, NJ.

My name was on the door, the letterhead, and business cards. Looking at it felt like success. It was about that time that I reached new, remarkable heights in my arrogant, self-exaggerated, "living legend" status. Even though God and I were getting to know one another and I was grateful he intervened with Tara, I had not fully committed to living my life for Him. For now, it was still pretty much about me.

As the new firm moved forward, I became a regular keynote speaker at gold shows and investment conferences worldwide. I was doing a lot of on-air and print media interviews, as well as my local TV show. At one investment conference, I met a man named Rick who came looking for someone to manage four hedge funds he and his partners were forming. He chose me and later started a new mutual fund that I managed and which bore my name, The Peter Grandich Contrarian Fund. I finally had a fund with my name on it. My head grew another two sizes. As far as my pompous self was concerned, I had hit the big time.

Despite the opportunity he afforded me, it became increasingly difficult to work with Rick. He was a brilliant but extremely demanding man. He was controlling and never left me alone. He'd call nights, weekends, even on Christmas Day. I felt a constant pressure to perform, which I just wasn't accustomed to. At the same time, I started marketing a small, select group of public companies and received fees and stock options for my work.

Of course, everything was disclosed. As a matter of fact, thanks to advice long ago from a wonderful attorney name Jerry Selvers, I have always disclosed so much information that people laughed at my disclaimer. But, Jerry taught me long ago that if you don't want to be sued and found guilty, there are three rules.

1.   Fully disclose.
2.   Fully disclose.
3.   Fully disclose.

"Tell them everything," Jerry would say, "Even if your disclaimer is longer than your commentary." It often was.

Around 1995, one of the companies I was doing marketing consulting for went from one dollar to nine dollars. Another went from two dollars to twelve dollars. I exercised my options, which were part of the disclosed compensation package, and cashed in big. It didn't take long to realize that I (and the firm) made more money on those two stocks than the grand total that I had made in the last several years combined. At the same time, it was becoming harder and harder to work with Rick, and the hedge funds and mutual fund were going nowhere fast. So consulting to these public companies really seemed like a no-brainer. That's when I decided to get out of the brokerage business altogether and turn my book over to one of my old partners from AFM. Since the fall-out, we had resolved our differences and became good friends again, and I announced that I was going full time into consulting and newsletter writing.

Chapter 5

... *Falling Down—and Up*

During this time in my life I was practicing what I have baptized as "Godfather Catholicism." In the movie *The Godfather*, Al Pacino was in church confessing his faith while at the same time having numerous crime bosses whacked. Like Pacino, I was going to church when it suited me, donating lots of money—mostly for show—yet not embracing my faith. I was too caught up in me and my greatness.

My life's priorities were something like this: Numero Uno was me, my reputation, and my ego. Then came Mary and Tara, and little else, especially God, was even in the picture. Though I went to church, it was more to make my wife happy than anything else. When I gave money, it was seeking praise and recognition for me and my business.

My net worth was in the seven figures, so naturally I had to buy lots of showy "stuff"—a multi-acre mini-estate, five racehorses, two stock cars—all with my name attached.

Soon, I took up a terrible male addiction: golf.

Now, I know that sounds funny to a lot of people, but it really was just that: an addiction. I went literally every single day to take lessons from a scratch golfer. I practiced constantly, and within a year went from the "typical" golfer score of 120 to hitting 90. Characteristic of everything else in my life that I did 110 percent or not at all (including sinning), golf became an obsession.

One day, Mary said, "You have played golf for nine days in a row." To which I responded, "It is my plan to play golf every day for the rest of my life."

Life was pretty sweet, or so I thought. I was making trades from the golf course, producing my newsletter, and traveling for speaking engagements and media interviews. I spent a lot of time and money at the track, spent hundreds of thousands on the horses I owned and betting, spent lots of cash on taking friends golfing, and lived life large.

I loved taking other people along for the ride and was always more comfortable with blue-collar folks. Even though I had significant wealth, I enjoyed much more being around regular guys than the Wharton types, probably because I just wasn't one of them. Because of my upbringing, I felt more real around working people. To me, they had no airs. What you saw was always what you got. Around these folks who were my friends, I wasn't the great Wall Street Whiz Kid, just Pete. But, I also think there was a part of me that thought I was the better man because I was the guy with the fame and they were the working stiffs.

Still, I had no real faith.

One night at a charity art auction, I met a man named Bill Wegner. Actually, I had met him earlier that day in church. Bill had been the Eucharistic minister and had served me communion. So, after the art auction, I approached him with my hands stretched out in front of me and said, "Does this remind you of anything?" Bill was puzzled and looked around as if checking for *Candid Camera*. I said, "You gave me communion a few hours ago." Bill later told me he thought I was a real weirdo, but despite that we became great friends.

Bill had been a very successful and prosperous businessman, community leader and elected official. A former schoolteacher turned hotel manager turned entrepreneur millionaire, he owned a national real estate company, an insurance agency, a travel agency, and a home development company. Eventually, however, he ended up losing just about everything and owing big (huge) money to the IRS. Although he was raised Catholic, he had not gone to church in twenty years. But, like Mary, Bill's wife was a devout Catholic and went to Mass regularly. Because of all of the business problems he had gone through, Bill went through some pretty tough times. He suffered tremendous panic attacks and fear, and eventually found his way back to the Church as a Catholic lay evangelist. He started a ministry called Good News International Ministries and travels around the world preaching and teaching about God's radical love. (I know that the term "Catholic evangelist" may sound like is an oxymoron to my Protestant brethren. Be careful, if the Catholics are evangelizing the end of the world can't be far behind.) We soon became close, close friends and golfing buddies.

I loved being with Bill. I had such admiration and love for him from the very start. And, from the moment we met it was one practical joke after another.

Bill often says, "Peter has a tremendous sense of humor, though he's nowhere near as funny as I am, but he thinks he is, and that's important."

As we golfed and joked (all the while Bill trying to bring me closer to the Church), I had no idea what a true blessing our friendship would become.

~~~

Remember that in between the fun and merrymaking, I was still "working." I was consulting mainly for mining and exploration companies and trading my own account.

Bre-x, a firm I *did not* work for, was a mining company that announced they found almost 200 million ounces of gold in Asia—an unheard-of amount. Their stock soared to near $200 a share. But, it turned out to be a total lie and the stock tanked.

Then, one of the guys who supposedly found the gold died suspiciously by falling out of a helicopter. That scandal, coupled with falling gold prices, really impacted the market. It was a rough time.

I decided that in order to protect the "kingdom" I had built I needed to buy shares in many of the companies I worked for. It was a really stupid move, but I thought it would show me to be a true "believer" in the companies. Ultimately, I put far more money into these than I should have, but I did it to protect my position as an "expert" and thereby protect my ego.

The market continued to unravel, and so did I. I worried ... a lot!

I worried so much that it literally made me sick. One day, Mary rushed me to hospital with what we were sure was a heart attack. There I lay in the emergency room hooked up to machines and tubes and wires for an hour as the doctors tried frantically to diagnose my chest pain, racing heart, anxiety, and shortness of breath. Mary prayed. I prayed a little, too, but worried a lot.

Finally, after about two hours, they sent in a psychiatrist who told me he thought I was having a panic attack, not a heart attack. A panic attack? Me? The great and powerful Wall Street Whiz Kid? He had to be wrong. I was pissed off.

Though it may sound insane, I wanted it to be a heart attack. There's no shame in a heart attack. Heck, they're standard operating procedure on Wall Street. Panic attacks, I thought, were for weak people. Imbalanced people. Panic attacks come from panic disorders, a psychological problem, and I was no wacko. Or so I thought.

Obviously, the doctor proved to be right, and I was suffering the first of a series of crippling and intense periods of anxiety and hopelessness in my life. I wasn't alone ... it is estimated that thirty million adult Americans will suffer from the disabling, unexpected and often unprovoked fear and pain of a panic attack sometime in their lives.

Though this first attack had severe physical symptoms, many times over the next year they came with a deep and sincere feeling of anxiety. I felt trapped, like I couldn't breathe. For no real or substantiated reason, I began to dread. Everything. Depression soon set in.

Then came the fear of providing for my family. The reality was that I had enough money in the bank to invest modestly and live off of for a very long time. But reality is of little importance when you are delusional. Whether realistic or unrealistic, I no longer felt I could live off of trading and working for these companies, and I suffered severe panic over how I could support my family and my lifestyle.

To make matters worse, the price of gold began to fall sharply and my "paper" value fell with it. Like a rock. It got pretty bad pretty fast. Suddenly I felt I had to get rid of all my worldly possessions and hunker down bracing for the worst. Gone were the horses, which cost thousands each month to care for and maintain. Then, I pulled my backing of the race cars. I feared that I would have to swallow my pride and go back to working in a brokerage office—the same humble beginning from which I had come. The shame of it just added to the panic and depression.

I cried. A lot. I mean, *really* a lot.

It was as if there was a big block in my head that was not letting reason in. For months and months, my days were dominated by fear and shame and a feeling of unworthiness. I feared going broke. With the Internet bubble growing, I feared (as many others had) that brokers would become obsolete and investors would do all their trading online, thus making brokers dinosaurs.

I feared what everyone would think. I had made it very well known that I was under fifty and semiretired. What did I do to my family? I could barely get out of bed.

Though I still had a few clients at that point, my income was less than my expenses, and my worth went from seven figures to six and it was still dropping.

Mary didn't understand. Though she truly tried, she'd never seen anything like this before. How could her strong, commanding, in-control husband go from being so on top of his game to crying and groveling and worrying about every little thing? It didn't help that I had kept her in the dark about most of the financial moves I had made. She never questioned; she let me do what made me happy. But it ended up making me truly miserable and she was bewildered by the whole thing.

At one point, I went to the beach near my home and walked across the bridge spanning the inlet. The fishing boats chugged out to sea beneath me as the waves crashed against the rocks. The air was still. For a moment, I contemplated jumping. That would solve everything, I thought. Mary would get the insurance money while she was still young and beautiful and able to remarry, and I would be out of my misery.

I peered over the edge at the rocks below. It was low tide and I could see the green algae and barnacles on the rocks. They looked slimy. The air at low tide smelled like bait left in the sun too long. I thought again about jumping, then realized that the bridge probably wasn't high enough. With my luck, I thought, I'd end up crippled for life, not dead. What a loser, I couldn't even kill myself.

At that precise moment a gust of wind came off the ocean and physically pushed me back away from the edge. It came from nowhere, or maybe it came from heaven. On this totally calm day I was almost knocked over by this gust of Godly air.

A sense of urgency came over me, and I hurried back to my car.

~~~

Finally, with nowhere else to turn, I turned to Bill. Not only had he been through bucket loads of his own crap, Bill had come through—he was a survivor of sorts. A compatriot in panic.

I went to Bill's home or office daily. We talked. We prayed. I cried. We just sat together sometimes. I came early in the morning and stayed until late at night. The next morning at 7 a.m. I was back. One time I remember him asking me if I had slept on the porch.

He was patient. He was firm, but kind. He was loving. He told me to look in the scriptures for my answers.

Sometime later, another friend was seeking Bill's advice on how to help me, and he told her, "After a while it doesn't matter what you say to Peter, it only matters that you are there for him. You just have to be there with him."

And Bill always was.

Today he tells the story of how at one point I wanted to send Mary and Tara off to live in Ireland, and I'd live in his garage. That's how "sound" my thinking was: The Wall Street Whiz Kid, with six figures in the bank, living in another man's garage. It was senseless.

I also spent a lot of time with Father Williams, the man who years before had healed Tara, a man I came to find out was one heck of a good golfer. Father prayed with me and guided me, and, like Bill, sent me to the Bible each day for answers.

Things just didn't seem as bad when I was with Bill and Father. When you're really scared, you learn that if you can get a break—even if only for an hour or two—it's something very special. The time I spent with Bill was just that: special.

When I was depressed and under excruciating anxiety, I could never honestly have a "good" time. So I tried each day to make my days "not totally horrible." What a thing to shoot for, huh? I did my best to surround myself with Christian friends; I went to Bible study, Mass, adoration ... any place where I felt God was present. I spent lots of hours in church.

Finally, after being dragged through the deepest of miseries, I started to believe in God on a real, daily basis. It's not like I had any other choice, mind you. Remember, I was totally without hope. As I read scripture, I saw that all of the evils the apostles described coming to sinners had come to me. I was a sinner ... and a big one, at that.

One day, I was just so physically and emotionally and mentally tired, I went to Bill and asked him to have me committed to a mental hospital. I could bear no more. I had hit rock bottom.

Bill complied, and as we drove to the facility I can remember him saying, "You won't believe this now, but this is going to turn out to be the greatest day of your life." Bill recognized that I was finally submitting myself to the Lord and realizing that I couldn't fix this myself, that only God could make this better. I had to give in to real help, real medicine, and real treatment.

It took years for me to agree, but he was so very right.

Bill will tell you that I only stayed a few hours. I called him up and said, "Get me outta here." I think I said something stupid like, "These people are really nuts. I'm not this crazy, I don't want to be in here."

Though I stayed less than a day, it was like a door opened. I had a reason to get better and I felt for the first time that I could do it with God's help.

~~~

Slowly, I began to do more little bits of work. As the new millennium came, I wrote a long detailed commentary about how the Internet bubble on Wall Street was going to burst and the stock market would cave. When I published it, I think I did it half for my readers and half for me.

In light of everything I saw coming down the road, I decided I couldn't keep up this high-net-worth lifestyle any longer. I was living way beyond my means (like most Americans) and if I was ever to have any real peace, I had to downsize. But, like everything else in my life, I did it 110 percent. We super-downsized!

Mary and I cleaned out the mini-estate and picked out a small condo in a new development under construction. It was small—modest, they say—and it gave me some peace.

As it turned out, the house sold quickly and the condo wasn't yet ready, so the Wall Street Whiz Kid packed up his family and a few belongings and moved into a motel on the highway. Though I was on the road to recovery it had been a long haul and I still was feeling the pangs of depression. Moving into a hotel for three months didn't help. I can remember that last night leaving the house was very emotional. When we got to the motel room Tara and Mary got in the bed with me, we all snuggled together and one of them said, "We'll be okay. Even if we have to sleep in cardboard boxes, as long as we are together everything will be okay."

Picture it. Imagine your wife and daughter telling that to you, the provider and head of the household. I remember crying about it a lot, but also having a sense of relief. At least I knew I would not lose my family, I would have a job, and I could start over again.

In that move we went from a 5,000-square-foot home on about six acres in one of the most prestigious communities to a 1,700-square-foot condominium on the third floor of a blue-collar neighborhood. I went from driving a Lincoln or Cadillac to driving a Chevy. The horses were gone, race cars were gone ... almost everything. (But I kept my golf clubs, thank God!)

An interesting thing happened in the process of downsizing. As we were preparing to move from the home, I held a garage sale to which a very aristocratic-looking (read that as "snooty") woman in a big fancy car drove up. The woman got out of her car and perused the many items we were unloading, including an organ that Tara had played. She inquired about the price of the organ, which I told her was fifty dollars. She scoffed, acting as if it was highly overpriced.

As she looked over the remaining items, we made small talk and she asked where I was moving. When I told her she was shocked and appalled. How could I move from this lovely town to that working-class community, she asked? She seemed almost disgusted. What an imbecile.

Almost as she drove away another car pulled up the long drive, smoke puffing from its tailpipe. Out of the car came a family that appeared to be of considerably less means—a lovely group of people who looked eagerly over my collection of sale items. They too, inquired about the organ. I thought for a moment about the woman who had just left and I told this family twenty dollars. Each member emptied his pockets until they scraped together the twenty bucks. Seeing how keen they were to have this for their child (and feeling like I needed to do a mitzvah) I told them to take it—no charge.

You'd have thought I gave them ten pounds of gold. They thanked me a dozen times and started carting it down the driveway to put in their old car. About the same time, the other lady pulled back in, presumably to make another bid for the organ, and saw this family stowing it in their vehicle. I could hear as she asked them how much they paid for it, and the family delightedly replied, "Nothing, he gave it to us for free."

Lady Number One was considerably angry. It made me smile.

That exchange made me realize that the presumed status I had in this high-net-worth community was really not as important as I had originally thought. In one very small way, it seemed to make the move a little easier.

I slowly started to come out of my funk.

Chapter 6

The Making of Trinity Financial

A friend of mine who owned New Jersey's largest business newspaper did a story on my rise and fall from financial grace titled, "Wall Street Whiz Kid Turns to Fizz." After the article hit, I received numerous calls with job offers. One of those calls was from a man named Frank Congilose.

Though I didn't remember having ever met him, Frank said he knew me from a local community group, and we arranged to meet at a little café to discuss my prospects. I was eager for work, healing, and a normal lifestyle. Coming into the meeting I was expecting your basic Wall Street-type interview, but what happened was a jaw-dropping experience for me. We sat for about two hours and in those 120 minutes he turned my world upside down. Frank showed me how just about everything I and most other Wall Street "professionals" had ever learned and practiced was a horribly flawed process. He blew a torpedo-sized hole in the very foundation of my financial knowledge and showed me that I had been going about financial planning all wrong. Dead wrong!

It started something like this: as I sat across from Frank, he leaned in as if he was telling me a deep, dark secret.

"Most people have been misguided into believing that success is defined by net worth and that the stock market will make them wealthy ... that they can *invest* their way into wealth," said Frank. "But that isn't true. The key to wealth is cash flow and investing in yourself and really building wealth and protecting your assets."

Then he sat back and let me absorb what he had said. *The key to wealth is cash flow.*

Whoa, I thought. You mean to tell me that investing in the market *won't* make you wealthy? C'mon. This went against everything—I mean *everything*—I had been taught and believed.

At first, I couldn't accept it—if it seems too good to be true, it must be, right? But, after meeting with Frank a few more times and really investigating the wealth-building principles he practiced, I found his way of doing business to be not only the real deal, but a Godly way to approach finances. I was sold. Within a short period of time, plans were solidified for me to start working at his company.

Over the years, through his friendship and teachings, Frank Congilose has been instrumental in helping me understand the flaws in much of traditional financial planning. Today, he is the founder of The Institute of Responsible Wealth, a New Jersey-based organization that helps people build and protect their wealth by focusing on five different areas of guidance: spiritual life, physical and mental health, family resources, business development, and professional resources. You will read more of his concepts in Chapter 12.

In late 1999, just as I was set to start working for Frank, I received an offer from a friend in Canada asking me to manage a new fund his firm was opening with a European bank in the Bahamas. At that point I wasn't really "looking," but it was a great offer. Hmmm, stay in New Jersey (cold, snow, lots of people) or move to the Bahamas (tropical paradise)? If only all decisions were that easy. So, I said thanks to Frank for the opportunity and went with the fund manager position.

Though I was excited about the opportunity, I never actually moved to the Bahamas. We were waiting for the money to come through from an Italian bank that was supposed to put a large chunk of capital into the fund, so I went down several times to look for office space and make plans. But after six or seven months the money never materialized, so I had to conclude that the fund failed and I was back where I was before: in New Jersey with panic attacks, depression and no job.

Actually, I was in worse shape than before. The thought of working in the Bahamas had really given me a psychological boost. It was certainly head and shoulders above going back to being a broker or learning a whole new business model with Frank. I was looking forward to it and it seemed like the new start that I needed. When it all fell apart I became even *more* depressed than I was seven months prior. I was devastated. The panic attacks came back with a vengeance.

Perhaps the most devastating was the thought of having to come crawling back to Frank. It was shameful; like I was starting all over again. How would I explain this to people?

With tail between my legs I met with Frank again and he graciously extended his job offer ... again. Of course, this time I took it and entered the new millennium a somewhat broken (but employed) man.

As I began working for Frank, I grew increasingly worried about the general stock market. The Internet was super hot and the NASDAQ was going up to the stratosphere. There were daily offerings of Internet-based IPOs that opened in the dollar range and by day's end were up to **ten** times that price. It was crazy. Everybody was coming out with an Internet-based company that was supposed to replace what humans used to do, factoring the value of the company's stock based on the number of "hits" the site got.

I'll never forget sitting in a clubhouse after a round of golf hearing two guys at the bar tell how they were going to make 20–30 percent in the NASDAQ in the next three years. They were so sure of it, and frankly, didn't want to hear anything to the contrary. My years in the business have given me the wisdom to know that when you hear statements like that, the bell has rung and it's too late. Well, that was about a month before the market peaked.

In an article I wrote for *Bull and Bear Magazine*, I stated that this mania was going to end in a bust shortly and the market would get creamed. At this point, I had sixteen years in the business and I had a legitimate sense of scrutiny of the markets. I had developed a system of analysis and saw what I thought were real fundamental, technical, and economic reasons why the market would fall. As if on cue, the market topped out in June and the NASDAQ lost 75 percent of its value.

Meanwhile, I was finally getting my head back on straight and this time around I began to get half serious about my faith. Previously, I was what I like to call a "C & E Catholic": one of the millions who goes to church on Christmas and Easter. But now I was attending church regularly, going to Bible study, reading scripture, and "fellowshipping" with other

Christians. Fellowshipping is Christian slang for hanging out and otherwise spending time with your Christian brethren. Understanding that your mother was right when she told you that you were probably going to become "like" the kids you hung out with, I opted to spend my time with like-minded Christian folk. It paid off. My faith grew.

I am not and have never been big on the Catholic versus Protestant debate. I don't believe we'll be wearing denomination labels in heaven so why get so caught up in it here on Earth? I would rather concentrate on the 85 or 90 percent that Catholics and Protestants share in their faith than the small minority they interpret differently. Therefore, I didn't just spend time with fellow Catholics, but Christians of all denominations. I still attended Mass, but also visited some Protestant churches and in fact, became quite close with a wonderful United Methodist preacher, Pastor Greg Bruton.

In 2000, around the time the market was tanking, I attended a local Christian businessmen's breakfast where I met Harry Flaherty. Harry is a retired football player who had played with the Philadelphia Eagles and Dallas Cowboys, and was now in charge of the New Jersey/New York chapter of the Fellowship of Christian Athletes. After a lunch meeting a short time later, I accepted a position on FCA's board of directors and began supporting the organization.

It was through my involvement with FCA (a great organization that sets up student chapters called "huddles" in public schools) that I soon met a man who would have a big impact on my life: former NY Giant Lee Rouson, who played on the team during its first two Super Bowl Championship seasons. Lee is also a gifted singer with a deep baritone voice and I've often heard him belt out gospel hymns—something you might not expect from his imposing persona. In 2008, just before the Giants went to the Super Bowl, he released the song "Go, Giants, Go." He currently worships and preaches at New Horizon Church in Harlem, NY.

When I told Lee about my background, he announced that I was the man he was looking for. He said God had led him to want to start a Christian-based financial services company geared toward professional athletes.

That's when I realized that God has a sense of humor. I told Lee he must be mistaken, because as a diehard NY Jets fan, "I used to root for players like you to drop the ball and die ... are you sure you want me?" He did.

Lee has said more than once that NFL should stand for "Not For Long" because when guys come into the league they are young, inexperienced, impressionable, and making huge money that doesn't last long. He had a real desire to offer advice, guidance, and support to these young players who, when left to the worldly system, are often left broke and broken after just a few years playing professional sports. His football experience and my investment knowhow seemed like a perfect fit.

So, with no formal business plan or even any real idea of how business would be done, in 2001 Lee and I started Trinity Financial Sports & Entertainment Management Company, LLC. Unfortunately, while Frank supported the idea, the companies Frank represented didn't. One guy, who said Trinity would never work, joked that "you can't put Jesus on the door."

After much prayer, I had to make the tough decision to leave Frank and his business and go out on my own. By late 2001, Trinity Financial consisted only of me and Lee.

~~~

Over the years, marketing professionals have told me I am the master of self-promotion and marketing. I don't know about that, but I do know that certain concepts just make sense to me. I guess I can see the big picture better than some others and I understand the value of good marketing and publicity.

It was with that future big picture in mind that I decided to build a high-profile corporate advisory board of current and former athletes and entertainers who would help give personal and professional advice to clients and lend credibility to my fledgling company. This, I thought, needed to be done before we started chasing down big-name clients. The search began.

The first to join my board in early 2002 was another former NY Giant whom I also met through my involvement in FCA, Keith Elias. Keith is somewhat of a local hero in New Jersey because he played high school, college, and pro ball all here in the Garden State. He is also one of those rare players who I've said I'd like to see marry my daughter. A Princeton graduate, he is a truly genuine guy who is as smart and good-looking as he is nice. Keith is also a humble man with a heart for God. He saw that our missions were aligned, and he came on board.

I remember thinking how amazing it was that God set all this up. I mean, it had to be God. How many people meet and get to know one pro football player, let alone two or three or dozens? God just kept putting the right people in my path. When some unreal scenario played out before me, I came to understand that it was God. Every time we came in contact with another pro player, I saw it as God fulfilling Lee's vision of offering financial advice to professional athletes—it was a gift from God to our business.

The next two athletes to join the board were pro wrestlers, Hawk and Animal—The Legion of Doom, The Road Warriors. Being a closet wrestling fan, I was elated when they agreed to serve on the board. Not long afterwards, I was so saddened when Hawk, a truly loving man of God, died suddenly.

Next, I met Michael Klecko, the son of my all-time favorite football player, Joe Klecko. Michael took me golfing with former boxing great "Gentleman Gerry" Cooney and, within eighteen holes of golf, Gerry offered to help me in any way he could. He, too, joined the board. Cooney, I must tell you, is truly a gentleman—it's easy to see how he got that name. He is also one of the funniest men I've ever met and shares my love of practical jokes.

Meanwhile, Michael told me that he and his father would be going to a healing Mass at St. Veronica's Church, and asked if I would like to come and meet his dad afterwards. Did I want to meet his dad? Oh, yeah! I'd almost give up my golf clubs to meet Joe Klecko! I don't want to say that I idolized Klecko because the Bible says idols are a big no-no, but—wow. Joe Klecko? I couldn't believe I was going to meet him.

When I lived in the Bronx we loved hard-hitting, working-class guys like Klecko. Growing up, my father would always say if there were ten other players like Joe the Jets would never lose a game. He was such a force. He never stopped and was very humble—a blue-collar guy. Along with Mark Gastineau, Abdul Salaam, and Marty Lyons, he co-anchored the notorious Jets "New York Sack Exchange" that racked up sixty-six sacks in the 1981 season alone. He is second only to Gastineau as the Jets' all-time sack leader, and in 2004 the Jets retired his number 73 jersey. He was one of only three guys to ever have his number retired by the Jets. I am still waiting for him to make the Hall of Fame.

I went to the Mass that night and took Keith Elias with me. Keith, a Protestant who had never been in a Catholic church, wanted to be prayed over for a shoulder injury that no one could seem to fix. The healing Mass was led by Father Williams, the same Godly man who presided over the Mass that healed Mary, and the man who helped me through my deep, dark depression. If all priests were like Father Williams, there would never be a negative word uttered about a Catholic priest. He is truly a wonderful, loving, Godly man.

Keith and I met at the church and walked in together just before the service began. Much to my surprise, there, just a few pews away, was Klecko. When it came time for people to be prayed over, Father asked for catchers and both Michael and Joe Klecko volunteered. Keith got in line to receive prayer and ended up being prayed over by Father. As often happens during these very moving and powerful services, and as had happened to my wife a few years earlier, Keith became slain in the Spirit, collapsed backwards into Joe Klecko's arms, and Klecko gently glided him to the ground.

When the service was over, I walked with everyone to the refreshment room and made my very first comment to my hero, Joe Klecko.

"After thirty years I was glad to see a Jet finally catch a Giant." The instant the words escaped from my mouth, I wanted to take them back. Oh, I wanted to curl up and die. What an idiot! Joe gave me one of those "Here's a crazy fan" looks, but he remained a gentleman.

Keith, incidentally, was totally healed of his injury that night.

In spite of the rocky start to our relationship, in the years that followed, Joe Klecko and I became very close friends.

Thanks to a legitimate introduction from Father Williams, Joe met with me privately and we just hit it off. Since then, our families have spent countless hours together, even vacationing together. Our children get along, our wives get along, and now we see each other at least once a week. But I am no longer enamored with Joe Klecko the football player, I am captivated by Joe Klecko the human being and devout Christian. To sit and watch a football game with him is remarkable because he sees things you don't see. He has an unbelievable knowledge of the game, which is likely why he is now an analyst on SNY Network's exclusive Jets TV coverage. When we first met in 2002, I had no idea how truly important our friendship would be. In my darkest days still to come, Joe would prove to be a true heaven-sent angel.

Other athletes who joined the board included NJ Devils hockey star Ken Daneyko; fifteen-year NFL veteran Dave Szott (now head of player personnel for the NY Jets); New York Giants Super Bowl hero David Tyree; NFL players Jay Feely, Reggie Hodges, and Chansi Stuckey; New York Rangers greats Ron Greschner and Nick Fotiu (who was just about as big of a sports hero to me as Klecko); as well as some very prominent businessmen. My good fortune in meeting athletes seemed to be on a roll.

Keith Elias introduced me to another Christian man with whom I would become very close, George McGovern. George is the area chapel leader for Athletes in Action and serves as chaplain for both the NY Yankees and NY Giants. One of the most genuine Christian men I have ever met, he invited me to participate with him at team chapels and events and eventually allowed me to become part of his team. Looking back, I can see how it was God's hand that made all this happen. How else could I have been given that trust to become part of an intimate, players-only inner circle like the

NY Giants and New York Yankees chapel and Bible study?

I asked George recently why he ever gave me that personal access to players and he said, "You had a story that I knew the players could identify with. You were an American success story—from rags to riches. You were for the most part uneducated, yet went on to become a successful businessman and Wall Street executive."

As he tells it, there are some real similarities between my background and rise to stardom and the catapult to fame that many players experience.

"More importantly, you had a heart to serve athletes without any strings attached. You weren't in it for what you could get out of it, but you truly wanted to serve the athletes," he said.

Peter has brought the perspective of a man of faith who is not a cleric or clergy member, but a businessman who tries hard to live out his faith in the context of his calling as a businessman.

The players really appreciate his frankness and his willingness to make himself vulnerable as a man. He is a man who has wrestled with temptations, doubts, and pride issues—he is very vulnerable, humble, and acknowledges times of depression, times of doubt, temptation, and doesn't hide behind a façade of 'holier than thou.'

—George McGovern
Chaplain, NY Giants and NY Yankees

My association with George, also a member of my advisory board, led to meeting numerous baseball and football players, trips to locker room, watching games on the sidelines ... any sports fan's dream come true. My walls are now filled with signed photos from players, yet I never tire of meeting athletes who are putting their celebrity to good use by using their fame to bring people to the Lord.

From a sports fan's one-sided point of view, one of the biggest transformations that came from my friendship with George was the slow transformation from green to blue. It took a few years, but I went from being a die-hard Jets fan to a Giants fan as well. Several of my friends wonder if it came down to the Jets versus the Giants, who would I root for? (They may find out! As we get set to publish this book the Jets play the Giants in the regular season on Christmas Eve 2011.) I always respond by saying I'm a Joe Klecko fan first; the Jets and Giants battle for second.

Chapter 7

Grandich Publications and the Electronic Media

The color of my jersey seemed to have little effect on my income. Even though Trinity Financial was a Registered Investment Advisor, this time I didn't manage any equity portfolios. I just didn't want to get back into the daily grind and all that greed. From 2001 to 2003, Trinity Financial did zero business, but boy, I had a great time hanging out with the athletes! I did go back working with Frank as an outside representative and we became and still remain very good friends.

It also became crystal clear to me that stocks should not be a person's first investment. For the most part, stocks only equate to riches for the people who sell the advice, not the vast majority of people who take the advice and put their hard-earned money behind it. Yet many clients don't believe that or simply don't want to hear it. I found that many people who play the market are greedy and inexperienced, and I clearly did not want to fight with clients to try to convince them the right things to do.

The market had been in a vicious bear cycle. Gold had tumbled to about $250. It was so cheap, in fact, that nobody could make money in gold; it cost more to get it out of the ground than the previously "precious" metal was worth. Thus, the junior resource market had all but shut down.

But by 2003, people were starting to think the worst was over, and there were signs technically that the bear market was ending and a new bull market beginning. Gold had turned the corner and was rising above $300.

In March, an old friend from Canada called to see if I would come up to Toronto and speak about the markets at a big dinner held during the PDAC conference, the world's biggest metals and mining show. Though it had been almost three years since my last speaking gig, I still had some name recognition, and since there wasn't much happening for me in the States, I went and ended up meeting many old friends from my days on the speaking circuit.

Two of the men I reconnected with were principals of the Hunter-Dickinson Group, one of the best mining and exploration teams in the world today. They said that if I came back to consulting they would hire me for two of their companies. Another gentleman said the same for three of his companies. I subsequently met with my securities attorney— perhaps the highest paid of all law specialties—to see if I could have the best of both worlds: operate and try to grow Trinity Financial as well as form a new company that could publish the Grandich Letter and through which I could work as a paid consultant. With certain conditions the answer was yes, and Grandich Publications, L.L.C. was born.

I had tried to enter the world of electronic newsletter publishing on October 29, 2002, with a brief update under the name *The Trinity Report*, but it was short-lived. After only a few issues I put *The Trinity Report* to bed and rekindled the *Grandich Letter*. The first reissue was published July 3, 2003.

Oh, how a couple of years can change an industry! Electronic publishing, e-mail and the Web made newsletter writing a breeze compared with its old-fashioned, printed ancestor. Instead of typing on an IBM Selectric or sending my text to a printer for pasteup and layout, I could sit in my pajamas and write out my thoughts. A few keystrokes later, it was on the Web and in the subscriber's in box. Not only could I get my thoughts out to subscribers and the media immediately, but I could also get feedback just as quickly.

I returned to publishing *North of the Border* on January 4, 2004, and the *Blue Chip and Income Report* came shortly thereafter. I eventually found, however, that incorporating all of the commentary and opinions under the banner of the *Grandich Letter* was much more concise and easiest for subscribers to follow. Soon, I abandoned the others to focus on the *Grandich Letter*.

In early 2004, less than a year after reissuing my flagship newsletter, the media really opened up to me again. I was featured several times a month in CBS and later Dow Jones & Company's *MarketWatch*, as well as in *Barron's*, *Dow Jones Newswire*, and the *Wall Street Journal Online*. On July 2, I was a featured guest on Canada's ROB-TV, which later became BNN (Business News Network), one of the finest financial broadcasts in the world today. That began a long-term relationship which I enjoyed because of the anchors' breadth of knowledge and their unbiased coverage of business and financial news. I also took on a regular column in the industry newspaper *The Prospector*. I was quoted in *The New York Times*, *CNN Money*, *New Man Magazine*, *Financial*

Post, Bloomberg.com, Korelin Economics Report, The Gold
Report.com, Financial Lifeline Radio, US News & World
Report, and many other print, broadcast, and electronic
media. In one month in the summer of 2009, I appeared on
both CNBC's The Kudlow Report and Neil Cavuto's Your
World on Fox. My Web and marketing consultants continue
to get a kick out of seeing my name come up in some financial
wire report in Chinese, Japanese, German, Italian, and other
languages. I assume they are quoting me properly but honestly
have no way of knowing.

My commentary took another technology leap in 2008
when the Grandich Letter moved from the slick, graphically
designed PDF to an online blog format. Though not as
pretty, the Web-based medium was super fast and accessible
to most everybody on the planet. More important to me,
blogging is easier for the "computer challenged" like me; it's
something I can do without the help of a designer, editor, or
tech assistant. Finally, I could comment instantaneously—
for better or for worse.

~~~

I had been through a lot since my last foray into the metals and
mining markets, so when I returned to public speaking I was a
different person. I was very frank with audiences and readers
about where I had been and what I had been up to. I didn't
hide the fact that I had been through a terrible depression
and major uphill battle. I also did not hide the fact that I
had another business, a Christian-based financial consulting
company, and at times I grayed the lines of communication
between the two audiences. Yes, I lost some readers over that.
But I believed an occasional reference to my faith was okay,
because that is such an important part of my life.

I accepted more speaking gigs, and soon found myself again the master of ceremonies at several Cambridge House conferences. Between the regular media attention and the regular speaking engagements, Grandich Publications took off.

Reaction from the vast majority of people was good. But, then there were the "nasty-grams." It is amazing what some people will take the time and energy to put into writing. The more horrific the accusations and threats, the less likely the e-mail sender was to attach his or her name to the message. I always found that a bit amusing.

I got the "tout" e-mails, too. Because I was paid by companies as a consultant, people called me everything from a liar to a prostitute. They accused me of saying good things about a client company only because the client paid me, and nothing could have been further from the truth. Even though I fully disclosed all positions, which was a lesson I learned years ago, and constantly warned that my advice should be viewed as biased, people found it necessary to threaten me, my family, and my good name. Some of it was just outrageous. The irony was that some other people would accuse me of not doing enough promotion!

What these misguided individuals didn't know about were the many, many companies that I turned down and would not work for because I didn't think they'd ever become producers. For every one I accepted, I turned down ten—no matter how much they offered me! There were also companies that fired me because I gave my honest opinion about their prospects, which were sometimes bleak.

Once, during one Friday interview on BNN, I said (as I have stated many times), "for every one junior resource company that succeeds and makes money, there will be dozens that don't. So, failure is the norm in the mining industry and you should plan to lose all or part of your investment." On Monday one of my client companies and I parted ways because they thought that I was too negative about the industry. Fact is, it was—and is—the truth.

At least a few companies that I was once involved with I found were not, in my opinion, skilled enough to bring their projects to fruition or the projects were not what they lead people to believe, so I resigned and have turned down all offers to work with them again. Once, I turned down a private placement stock offering because I didn't think it was on the up-and-up, only to be told I wasn't a "player" and then terminated by the company. I was through with operating in the gray area: I did everything I could to do the right thing and offer what I felt was unbiased, solid commentary.

It's ironic that many of my so-called colleagues make deals behind the scenes like private placements that are never disclosed—deals about which investors will never know. There are newsletter writers who have arrangements to speak about a company and in return the company spends a few hundred thousand dollars to build the newsletter's subscriber base. Although that may not be "illegal," it is questionable at best and most would view it as immoral. I have made it a habit to disclose all compensations and positions, and I have always been very choosy about to which companies I will lend my name. Some other "experts" are just paid mouthpieces; you just don't know it. See for yourself how many newsletter writers fully disclose their positions and potential conflicts of interest. But please know that there are some very honorable people, as well.

In addition to writing about companies, whether or not I

had a stake in them, I wrote about my often contrarian views of the markets, economies, and geopolitical concerns. I also publish a tracking list of individual stocks I personally find attractive. There's no subscription cost for my blog, and never a requirement that a reader had to read my company comments in order to receive the market and economic commentary. Besides, you can click "REMOVE" at any time.

To borrow a term from my newsletters and my blog, the *Bottomline* is this: I know that if I give up my integrity, nobody will be interested to hear what I have to say ... not subscribers, not companies, not the media. That's why I have always worked hard to be associated only with companies I feel strongly about; to protect my name and my image with 100 percent disclosure. I've made it crystal clear that failure is the norm in the junior resource game and one is gambling, not speculating, and needs to be fully prepared to lose part or all of their capital.

~~~

As Grandich Publications grew, I traveled, wined-and-dined, and found success for a miraculous second time in my life. I paid little attention to Trinity Financial as a business, but I did use it for a host of philanthropic gestures, as well as stroking my ego by meeting many professional athletes and being seen with them. From 2003 through January 2008, I was on top of the world. It was truly the best of times. I was making serious money publishing my newsletters, speaking around the globe and trading to the point that my wealth grew even more than where it reached before things turned bad in 1999.

I believe I have spoken on just about every continent—South America, the Caribbean, Mexico, Europe, Africa, and several

Canadian cities—and too many cities in the U.S. to mention. With all the travelling I have done, there isn't a place I don't like except perhaps Paris. Travel, which had once been a perk of the business, became a real drag after September 11, 2001, for obvious and necessary reasons. Before 9/11, you could show up half an hour before takeoff. Today, lines are long, delays are the norm, there are fewer nonstops, and tempers run high. But there are still some bright spots to traveling like Vancouver!

Though I like Toronto very much, Vancouver is my favorite destination. I always have a good time in that beautiful city filled with friendly people. Toronto runs a close second, but the water and mountains from downtown Vancouver are just so beautiful.

Chapter 8

Drowning Again

One cold day in February 2008, I awoke to find that I had a very serious illness: depression. Much to my shock and horror, it came out of nowhere and gripped me hard to the point that I was suicidal. I tried to keep the details of my health private for fear my clients would let me go thinking I was unable to work. Rumors were circulating on the Internet that I was battling cancer—scuttlebutt that started in a chat room, no doubt. I didn't have cancer, but I neither confirmed nor denied. To be honest, cancer seemed a much more noble disease. So I let the rumors fly and simply had Jo Schloeder, my marketing consultant and friend, run interference with the companies, passing on vague messages and putting off commitments.

But I was about to face the most devastating six-month battle of my life. This time I wouldn't just think about doing myself in; I'd actually try.

~~~

To explain depression—to really and truly describe this illness that swallowed me up for another six months of my life—to someone who has never experienced it is like me trying to tell you what childbirth feels like. Unless you've been through it yourself it is nearly impossible to explain. Though I was with Mary through her contractions and labor and ultimate delivery of Tara, I can only tell you what I observed. I obviously can't know exactly how it felt.

It's the same with depression. If you have not personally experienced the fear and overwhelming helplessness of clinical depression—and I pray you never do—I don't know if you will be able to really grasp what I went through. But I'll try to explain it the best I can.

Remember, I began to aggressively warn my readers in 2007 that "America had been robbing Peter to pay Paul, and Peter is tapped out." I pounded the table in 2007 that the U.S. stock market wouldn't top out until the Federal Reserve Bank began easing monetary policy. They did in October of 2007 and I issued my most bearish forecast ever, titled, "Man Your Battle Stations." I envisioned the worst economic and stock market fall since the Great Depression.

In January 2008, I was in Vancouver for a conference and a few media appearances and I came down with a bad case of bronchitis. I was really sick. Coming home on the plane was gruesome for me. For weeks it dragged on, but I finally felt better by the time the Super Bowl came around because the New York Giants were in the big game. Having spent time with many of these guys in the locker room and Bible study, their pending success made me smile briefly.

However, shortly after the Super Bowl, a combination of my

health and the grim markets really began to plague me and I started suffering from anxiety. It wasn't depression, but stress and anxiety, which Joe Klecko joked was due to a lack of football. But the worry and apprehension quickly worsened and one day in February I awoke *paralyzed*. Not from some horrific spinal injury, but depression. I was essentially physically and mentally paralyzed by fear and a sense of total and utter lack of hope.

I would learn I was quite ill. This led me to spend days and weeks on end in my bedroom, venturing out only when I was forced to go to the doctor or therapist. I had motivation for nothing—not showering, shaving, eating, working, watching television, nothing. I stayed in my bed for hours, then days, simply crying uncontrollably at the mess I thought I had made of my life and the lives of my wife and daughter.

Though I had gone through panic attacks and depression before, this time it was different. It was debilitating. Last go 'round I spent days with Father Williams and Bill Wegner seeking comfort and slowly pulled out of it. This time, however, I stayed inside in the dark—like an agoraphobic frozen by the thought of being around people. The Devil had his hands around my throat and my heart and was squeezing the life from every single breath I took.

Then came the fatigue, the hours and hours of sleeping, followed by the inability to sleep at all. There was no escape from the impending doom I foresaw. I withdrew from everything. The simplest of tasks seemed unfathomable.

It was as if a truck was parked on my chest. I simply could not move. Sadness gripped me, swept me up, engulfed me and drowned my every moment. No matter how hard I tried, I just couldn't control my thoughts; negative, irrational, utterly

81

nonsensical thoughts consumed my every waking moment.
I had to stay away from my computer because the news in
the U.S. and around the world made me perceive everything
to be far worse. I sent cryptic messages to clients and readers
through Jo about the fact that I was "undergoing tests" and
"under doctor's orders." That certainly wasn't a lie because in
the beginning I really had a potential fatal ailment.

Though I didn't lie about my condition, I was afraid to tell
people what I was really dealing with. First, because at that
point I didn't think I would ever recover. And second, there
was the notion that admitting that I was battling depression
would brand me as being weak or emotional. (This from
the man who cried and cried in front of family, friends, and
complete strangers.)

My perception of the world was that I was a total failure.
Guilt set in.

On February 25, Jo, the only other person to ever post on my
blog, sent this message to my clients:

*Peter Grandich has been ill for the past several weeks,
starting on January 14th in Vancouver and recurring twice
since then, including this weekend. As a result, his immune
system became so depleted that he ended up in the hospital
Sunday and was kept overnight. He has been ordered to
stay on complete bed rest for at least the next 7–10 days,
as he is nearing severe exhaustion. Regretfully, per doctor's
orders he'll have to cancel his trip to Toronto this weekend.*

*Peter asked me to express his sincere gratitude to all of you
who he knows will be praying for his recovery, and wanted
me to assure you that in relatively short order (after some
much-needed rest) he'll be as good as new. Although he*

truly appreciates knowing that you are thinking of him, please don't send any gifts or flowers.

For the time being, Peter will not be responding to phone messages or e-mail. If you need to speak with him, please e-mail me as I will be in touch with him once daily.

To my great surprise, I got a lot of very positive emails via Jo. Dozens of messages and phone calls came in to her from clients, members of the media, and business associates. One e-mail said, "Just let Peter know that he is in my prayers, and that the drop in the price of gold is not a personal challenge from God just for him."

Everyone wished me a quick recovery, but I couldn't envision getting better; I was mad at myself. I thought despite telling everyone to sell everything and even go short, by staying with the junior resource stocks I was hurting many people and myself. Because of what I saw happening in the economy, I knew a major economic recession was coming, and how would I support my family?

On March 24, I wrote a friend and said,

The antidepressants made me sick as a dog. Will try another one. Trying to hold on but I'm scared I screwed up my whole life being aligned in this mining business. Can't make any real money elsewhere.

Then on April 2, I sent an email that started with,

I'm writing to my dearest friends on my 52nd birthday. I wish it was 72 as I would be closer to meeting my maker ... I so much want to meet my maker and spend eternity with him.

Five days later I emailed Jo:

I put my family behind the eight ball.

I realize the majority of the money I made these last few years has been from gambling on stocks.

Being a broker again has passed by as starting to build a book of business would be costly, timely, and I don't think the next several years will be great times so no matter what I said in the past, isn't going to drive people to me.

Mary doesn't realize any of this and already is very mad.

Yes, I have a so-called bankroll, but what do I do, sit and wait to die? And since I don't seem prepared to drive a limo for the rest of my natural life, I have no real hope. And the worst part is suicide is certain damnation.

Pretty good for the Wall Street Whiz Kid which was also b.s. Turns out most of my life was deceit and selfishness.

Now don't go calling Mary because I'm not about to jump off a bridge—yet. But outside of a miracle of miracles I ruined 3 lives—2 good ones and one lousy one, mine.

I was serious about driving a limo. I thought it was the only thing I was qualified to do. I also toyed with the idea of being a car salesman, but was told that I was overqualified for that. Oh, God, I couldn't even sell cars!

I know how unrealistic all of this must sound. Clearly, I had a thriving business and enough money in the bank to live comfortably for the rest of my life. I had no debt. I had a loving wife and daughter. Aside from an ailment that many people successfully overcome, and a few extra pounds, I had a great life. I had the ability to continue to provide for my family and I could even play golf several times a week.

To balanced, level people like my wife and many of my friends, they couldn't understand why I couldn't just "snap out of it." Get over it. They told me over and over how irrational I was being. But what they didn't and couldn't know was that "rational" thoughts as we know them are not part of a depressed person's thinking ability. Your doomsday thoughts are programmed by the sickness and there is no "rational."

There was a constant, unbreakable feeling of sadness, hopelessness, worthlessness, and eventually suicide. Ultimately, life just didn't seem worth living, and I told myself that Mary and Tara would be better off without me.

One morning in April, while Mary and Tara were in Ireland, I awoke feeling I just couldn't live anymore. I wrote Mary a long letter explaining all the financials and why I couldn't live. Then I wrote another letter, this time a goodbye note to Bill Wegner, who had been my most faithful friend. I was taking Xanax at the time, so I loaded a jarful in my pocket and headed down to Bill's office at St. Veronica's Church to give him the note.

For good or bad, Bill was out at the time, so I handed the note to the secretary and headed back to my car and started downing pills. I had taken six or eight of them by the time she followed me out and took the bottle, and within minutes Bill had called the police and I was admitted to a specialized psychiatric hospital.

It was almost like prison. For the first time in my life, I was locked up. I couldn't leave; in fact, I couldn't even leave the floor for the first two days, and then the farthest I could go was to walk around the grounds.

Everybody at this place had a problem—big problems. Some were addicts, there was a teacher who was cutting herself, and others were suicidal, like me. I felt extreme compassion for these patients and at times felt like my life wasn't nearly as bad, yet I remained full of fear.

Because I had already gone through psychotherapy and a number of different drug therapies, the doctors decided my only hope was electroconvulsive therapy, a k a electric shock therapy. It is as barbaric as it sounds: they plug you in and shoot electric current into your body until it convulses and you can't talk or think. It was debilitating. Painful. The plan was to have three rounds a day of this torture for four days, but after day one I couldn't even walk.

That's when I decided the therapy wasn't working. Since I had been there long enough I was able to check myself out, and I did, pronto. I couldn't deal with the thought of my wife or daughter seeing me there, so I called Bill to pick me up.

On that day, I returned home still a broken man and immediately returned to the lifestyle of crying, fear, loathing, and remorse. I'd later find out that although depression is more prevalent in women, men are four times more likely to kill themselves. So it made sense that I would try again.

The next time Mary and Tara were out of town, I attempted for a second time to take my life, this time by drinking and taking pills. However, my sister, who called in the midst of my self-destruction, thwarted my efforts by calling Bill who called the police again.

This time they took me to a community hospital psych ward where there were some really tough cases. Some were very, very mentally ill. I struck up a relationship with a young man who was there because, though he worked, he also drank and had been tossed out of where he lived and had no place to go. He was homeless. I had about eighteen bucks in my pocket, and the day I was released I gave it to him. The guy cried as if I had given him a million dollars.

"You know, no one's ever done this for me, no family, no nothing," he said.

"It's only eighteen dollars," I replied.

"It ain't the eighteen dollars," he said.

At that moment, even though I was so deeply depressed and suicidal, I could see the differences in his life and mine. I wept. And on the way home in the car with Bill I realized that though I was miserable and things seemed very bad, I could no longer just sit home wallowing in my fear and agony; I had to do something to occupy my mind.

Friends like Joe Klecko reinforced this. Time after time as I sat in Joe's living room he would preach to me about how life isn't just about money ... and it's not about me. It's God's. It's ALL God's. He tried to convince me of all that I had going for me and all that I had to be thankful for. And he gave me all the reasons why I should trust in God. I listened. Maybe I even believed him a little.

Remember that before getting sick, I sent out up to five *Grandich Letters* or *Special Alerts* a week. But from March through May I sent out a few brief paragraphs. Any time I felt well enough to write a few lines I would in an attempt to show my clients I was still alive.

In April I wrote to a colleague, "My return will likely not be seen for a while and please God not never." Then a few days later I also sent this to a few close friends:

Over these last several weeks, I've discovered how badly I've lived my life through total selfishness, pride, and sinfulness. My friend Joe Klecko really gave it to me in a good way yesterday showing me it's all about me and money, not trusting God. I went so far as to think I can drive a limo and discovered you make only $500–600 and have to be available 72 hours a week. Bottomline, there's nothing out there in any new field that I can make a living at.

God visited my bedroom last night at 3 a.m. and showed me besides all this, I've been a lazy worker and a quitter versus a fighter. I don't think this was the Devil because it wasn't with malice, but who knows.

I felt lost again and dragged myself with all my fears to church this morning. While sitting there, I saw a man who I've noticed there for the last two months. After church, I introduced myself and we began to talk. He ended up telling me he was 37 years old, had two children and a wife who doesn't work, was almost bankrupt, and last July was prepared to kill himself. He came to church after not being a religious person and felt he had to try his business again. He described how while he's still in hock he isn't depressed anymore and has stopped medicine and therapy. I told him a little about me and he ended up saying I should try to do whatever it seemed God had blessed me with. I told him it seems to be to talk about investments, economy but then gave him a long list of how that business has passed me by, etc. He absolutely urged me to go at it again as it has to be what God gave you as a gift—even if you didn't use it right in the past. I told him there seem to be a lot of obstacles to do it, including the fear of failure and ability, and he said is there anything else you could do and of course the answer was no.

Is this God speaking to me? I'm supposed to do His will. Could His will be for me not to try this again?

Trying to hold onto my money is only going to kill me over time. I'm scared to death, hard to think but want to share with my closes friends who could give me their insight.

After sending this email, Frank Congilose tried hard to make me see things rationally. He pulled me in his office one day and said, "Let's take a real look at your situation."

And he went line by line asking questions with me answering. "How much money do you have?"

"Millions," I murmured.

He said, "Are you married?"

"Yeah."

"Marriage happy?"

"Yeah."

"Child. Child okay?

"Yes."

"Do you owe anybody any money?"

"No."

"That means you own where you live, your cars, and everybody is healthy. You realize that your net worth puts you in the top 3 to 5 percent in America?"

Then he said, "What do you think, God is just going to shut it off now? You're never going to earn another dime again? Come on, that's stupid."

He said, "Do you really think that if you just came back here, went and got your license and started talking to people, you wouldn't do *any* business?" And he said, "Besides, you could easily not work for the next ten or fifteen years, as long as there is no major disaster. You know that most of the people we see, they have little or no savings, six months and..." he trailed off.

"So stop it," he concluded.

About the same time Frank was beating me up, so was Klecko. He pounded me about having to totally trust God, to give everything up to Him, and realize that it is all His anyway. Everything we do has to be in line with what God wants, Joe would tell me. He'd say that it's hard to stay focused on the Lord, but it comes with prayer, constant prayer.

~~~

I now know that depression is caused by genetic, biochemical, psychological, and environmental factors. Most notably, it is brought on by stress, trauma, and a chemical change in the brain that affects how the brain functions. I won't go into details but when millions of nerve cells called neurotransmitters don't function properly, the results can be deadly. To compound matters, depression can often run in families, and I learned that my father and all his family members and their children suffered from depression for many years.

It's been reported that over 18 million Americans suffer from depression, though I think that number may be way off because of the high number of unreported cases from people who either cannot afford to seek help or just don't. According to the National Institute of Health, major depressive disorder is the leading cause of disability in the U.S. for people ages 15–44.

Though we all throw around the term "depressing" from time to time, trust me when I tell you that true clinical depression is something you wouldn't wish upon your worst enemy.

It's an illness, and thankfully for me, it was a treatable one.

~~~

Unlike my first bout with depression, which took months to emerge from, this time it was like somebody flipped the switch and turned it off.

On August 29, a little more than six months after my living hell began, I received an e-mail from a friend that changed my outlook. Often throughout my illness, my friends would send me motivational messages, but this one was a link to a YouTube video called "That's My King." I don't know why, but I clicked to watch it.

By following a link to the Igniter Media Group website, I now know that the audio is of a service delivered by the late S.M. Lockridge, who delivered "an incredible message, describing our God and who He is. Though God can't be described with just words, this is as close as you can get this side of Heaven."

Dr. Shadrach Mesach (S.M.) Lockridge was the Pastor of Calvary Baptist Church in San Diego, California and was active in the civil rights movement.

The moving audio, in which Lockridge barks out again and again, "That's my King!" is accompanied by religious images that depict Jesus Christ. Lockridge asks over and over, "Do you know Him?" He describes how Jesus Christ supplies our strength, how He saves us, how He blesses us, and rewards us. Lockridge asks again and again, "Do you know Him? His mercy is everlasting, His love never changes, His yoke is easy, His burden is light. He's invincible. That's MY KING!"

Well, I watched that video and it was as if God himself reached down from Heaven and flipped the switch. I just bawled. And cried some more. Not crying out of fear or agony this time, but tears of joy—I was full of emotion and felt as if the Holy Spirit went through my whole body. I just knew that all the things the pastor said in that video were true. That God is everything, everywhere. It just hit me that I had to surrender. People like Joe Klecko and Bill Wegner had been telling me the same thing for months, imploring me to totally trust God. Somehow when they told me it didn't mean as much as when S.M. Lockridge, a pastor now dead, told me.

Mary and Tara were due home from Ireland and I didn't want them to see their father and husband in the bed crying anymore. So, that very day I got down on the floor and prayed. I called out to God and praised Him. My heart was full of joy. I know that sounds clichéd, but there is no other way to describe joy in your heart. I had a sense of warmness come over me. In fact, I was so warm I took my temperature because I thought I had a fever.

Later, I went to church and just sat for an hour thanking God.

The next morning, I had breakfast with George McGovern who prayed over me, and I had that great warm feeling again, just like I did as Father Williams has prayed over me. And I concluded that I had to get up and get to work. My potentially deadly illness was gone and my mind was clear and upbeat again.

It was an unbelievable journey. The feeling inside was like I finally allowed the Holy Spirit to come alive. Like I was finally allowing Him to operate within me.

HE flipped that switch.

~~~

When you're depressed, you get a knot in your head and can't think, and anytime you try to think, no matter what you think, you come up with a bad conclusion so that you don't think it can work. To truly overcome it, you need a combination of prayer, therapy, and medicine.

From my experience, I learned that Jesus is the ultimate answer. One person said to me, if you take one step and trust Him, he'll take a thousand, and that's what happened ever since then. I really think this was the first time that I had a real, true, purely personal relationship with Jesus. Although I may have appeared to be a Godly man before, in the past it was some of Him, and a lot of me. I had a "fair weather" relationship with the Lord. When things were good, I was willing to do all the things Jesus called me to do, especially on a generosity side. I always loved giving money to people and causes. It made me feel good. (My father was that way; he never had any money, but he was the most generous man you'd ever meet.)

But when things turned, I didn't have real trust in Him. I allowed the other one that roams the earth seeking to destroy to enter my mind and I listened to his lies and deceit. In my opinion, there are only two true emotions in the world: love, which comes from Jesus; and fear, which is of the devil.

When things went bad in the past, I didn't love Jesus—I called Him as if I was dialing 911. "Hello, Jesus, can you fix this?" I never said, "I love you, whatever you have planned I'll accept." That was the difference this time ... because I truly accepted His will that morning, and said whatever I have to do, even if it's not what I want to do, I'll do it.

The future? I'm taking it one day at a time.

Chapter 9

Christianity: What It Means to Me

As I said in the last chapter, I believe there are only two true human emotions: Love and Fear. Every other emotion is just a variation of love or fear. Jesus is all love. Satan is all fear. The problem that both believers and nonbelievers share is we spend too much time in the fear camp and not enough in the love camp.

I understand, as I am sure you do, that not all fear is bad. There are healthy fears like asking someone on a first date, fearing dangerous

No passion so effectually robs the mind of all its powers of acting and reasoning as fear.

—Edmund Burke (1729–1797)

situations, or even being fearful before making a speech. But fears like these usually end up being a positive because they raise your energy level and concentration on the task at hand. They help motivate you or help you avoid situations that could put you in harm's way.

Another "good" fear is fear of the Lord. It's not really about being afraid, but about respecting God. It is an awe of Him; a respect or reverence for His mightiness. Fear of the Lord is a good thing, and the Bible says, "The fear [or respect] of the Lord is the beginning of wisdom (Psalm 111:10)." And the book of Proverbs says, "The fear of the Lord is the beginning of knowledge (Proverbs 1:7)."

Destructive fear—the Satan kind of fear—is what the Bible calls "the spirit of fear." It is what the Devil and his demonic forces put in our lives at one time or another to make us question God. He tries to paralyze us so we don't fulfill what God has planned for us, and make us turn away from God as if He's let us down or deserted us.

This fear is not of God, it is a tool of Satan. We know that because in II Timothy 1:7, the Bible says, "For God has not given us a spirit of fear, but of power and love and a sound mind."

During my depths of depression when I felt life was not worth living, my mind was so full of fear that my friends told me I was being totally irrational. But Satan's fear is not rational. He's a big liar and he's quite convincing. When that spirit of fear tries to take over, as Christians we have to remember how much God loves us, and that we need to trust Him. "There is no fear in love," says I John 4:18, "But perfect love drives out fear."

For me, life as a Christian has come down to this: I must submit to either walking with God in _all_ His ways or not. If not, I allow the Devil to influence my life. Either you walk with the *Lord* or with *Satan*, it's that simple. Though you will not be perfect every single minute of every day, the choice is one or the other. There is no gray area here.

Whenever I have truly allowed God to lead me and I have fully concentrated on His will, which has not been often, life has been truly blessed. It was when I decided to go it alone and work from my own strength and sin that the Devil had me.

Though you have likely heard this many times before, I am constantly reminded that F.E.A.R. is just an acronym for False Evidence Appearing Real. Think about that for a moment: the terror and dread of fear is nothing more than phony, made-up facts that seem very, very real but are not. They're fake; like a very believable bad joke somebody is playing on you.

How do we know this to be so? Because the Bible says, "Do not fear, for I am with you; do not anxiously look about you, for I am your God. I will strengthen you (Isaiah 41:10)."

The fact is very simple: you cannot have both fear and the love of Jesus in your heart at the same time. It's one or the other; all or nothing. Christ's love pushes out, squashes, and rids you of the spirit of fear.

I have since come to learn that when fear strikes—and it will—we must do several things. First, ask ourselves what is behind this latest bout of fear? Is our fear rational? Have we had it before, and what were the results?

Next, look the fear straight in the eye and ask it, "What are you trying to tell me?" Get help both medically and spiritually.

Finally, accept it. With prayer and growing in faith in Jesus Christ, He will take away the fear if you ask Him to.

I am the world's worst cold caller. I hate rejection. You'll recall that I started my first investment newsletter partly because of my fear of cold calling. Only after my business was built up did the fear of rejection subside and confidence finally take over, to the point of arrogance at times. Fear of rejection is the greatest obstacle to a successful career. I'm no psychotherapist, though I've seen a few, but I believe those of us who fear failure and success were victims of destructive criticism as children and didn't get nourishing love. I know that's how it was for me, and I suspect it's the case for many.

True peace for me came only when I totally surrendered to Jesus. This finally came after six months of Joe Klecko urging me to act as if Jesus was standing at my front door asking to take away all my worries. Finally, I let Him.

If one passage of scripture can convince you to trust Jesus whenever fear grips you, it is Matthew 6:25–34, which says:

> Therefore I tell you, do not worry about your life, what you will eat or drink; or about your body, what you will wear. Is not life more important than food, and the body more important than clothes? Look at the birds of the air; they do not sow or reap or store away in barns, and yet your heavenly Father feeds them. Are you not much more valuable than they?

> Who of you by worrying can add a single hour to his life? And why do you worry about clothes? See how the lilies of the field grow. They do not labor or spin...

> So do not worry, saying, "What shall we eat?" or "What shall we drink?" or "What shall we wear?"

> For the pagans run after all these things, and your

heavenly Father knows that you need them. But seek first His kingdom and His righteousness, and all these things will be given to you as well.

Therefore do not worry about tomorrow, for tomorrow will worry about itself. Each day has enough trouble of its own.

~~~

I've had a lot to say about fear, now a few powerful words about love: it never fails.

1 Corinthians 13:4–8 says, "Love is patient, love is kind. It does not envy, it does not boast, it is not proud. It is not rude, it is not self-seeking, it is not easily angered, it keeps no record of wrongs. Love does not delight in evil but rejoices with the truth. It always protects, always trusts, always hopes, always perseveres. **Love never fails**."

As I said earlier, Jesus is love. Sounds like a bumper sticker, doesn't it? It's short and sweet, and it's so very, very true.

The Bible tells us that Jesus demonstrated *agape*—the Greek word for unconditional, self-sacrificing love. Not devotion or physical love or brotherly love or charity or friendship, but total unconditional love that can only be of and from God. Divine love.

The Apostle John wrote in I John 4:8, "God is love." Notice he doesn't say that God loves, but He *is* love. Everything He does is of His love. He loves those whom others can't or won't. It is His very nature to love.

The whole point of *agape* love is that we never did anything to deserve His love, yet He loves us anyway. And no matter what we do, He will always love us. He loves us so much that He sent his only child, His son Jesus, to be martyred, murdered, and die for us so we could live in heaven with Him. How could we ever deserve love like that? The answer is simply, we couldn't. There's nothing we could ever do to earn or justify *agape* love. Yet we have it.

> If you have it [love], you don't need to have anything else, and if you don't have it, it doesn't matter much what else you have.
>
> —Sir James M. Barrie

~~~

I receive mixed reviews when I share my faith in my business life. I fully respect those who choose not to believe. However, I'm like a person who saw the greatest movie or ate at the finest restaurant and just wants to tell everybody about it. I'm excited about God!

How do I know He exists? It's simple, at least, to me it is. I have faith, and by definition faith is belief and trust in something for which there is no "proof." Complete trust. The very word comes from the Latin *fidere* which means trust. "Faith is the substance of things hoped for, the evidence of things not seen," the Bible says in Hebrews 11:1.

Yet, to someone who doesn't want to believe there is a God, they can rationalize away any argument I put forth. Just like telling someone the earth is round, if he really and truly believes the Earth to be flat, no matter of documentation or proof can change his mind.

Here are some things to consider if you question, "Is there a God?"

Look at the Earth.

The universe displays such awesome and amazing design there must be a "designer." The Earth is perfect in its size and proportion, allowing for a thin layer of nitrogen and oxygen gasses to extend for about fifty miles beyond the planet's surface. If it were a little bit smaller, like the planet Mercury, for example, we would not have an atmosphere. If it were a little larger, like Jupiter, our atmosphere would contain free hydrogen. Of all the known planets, Earth is the only one with just the right mix of gases to support human, animal, and plant life.

Furthermore, our location from the sun is perfect. Any closer, and we'd roast. Any further, and we'd freeze. Even a slight variation in our location from the sun would make life on Earth unsustainable.

These circumstances didn't just happen randomly. Our Earth and everything around it was designed by God. *That* is the definition of awesome.

Did all this happen by chance?

If God does not exist, then the only explanation for our Earth, moon, water, air—all of it—is that it was just a random occurrence that happened by chance. Unpredictable luck. A couple of atoms smash together and *voilá*, there's the solar system. Sorry, I just can't buy that. Science proved many years ago that life cannot arise from nonlife. So, where did the first life form come from? What was the first being from which all others "evolved?" The chicken or the egg?

How about the millions of people who believe?

What about all the millions and millions of Christians who for centuries have had a written explanation of how the world came about? The *Holy Bible* is the best-selling book of all time and has been translated into every language on Earth. Could all those people be wrong? I guess it's possible, but highly unlikely. Either you believe the Bible is the Word of God, or you don't. Yes, it was written by his disciples and apostles over many years, but I know that the words in the Bible came from God. In II Timothy chapter 3, it says that "all scripture is God-breathed."

Though the Bible may be seventy-three different books written on three continents in three different languages over a period of roughly fifteen hundred years by more than forty authors, it is one cohesive book from beginning to end. Furthermore, it is historically accurate. Archeological evidence and other writings all prove the accuracy of the historical accounts of the Bible. It is, in fact, the best written account of the ancient world. Why, then, would the authors record history so accurately and with great detail and all the "God stuff" be made up?

~~~

It's interesting that polls show roughly 90 percent of the world's population believes in God or another higher power. So why isn't the burden of proof placed on the 10 percent who don't believe? Because those who don't want to believe never will no matter what proof is put before them. And those of us who do believe want so desperately to share the love we feel with others.

The *Bottomline* is that God can't be proven or disproven. His existence is simply a matter of faith—you know, "the substance of things hoped for, the evidence of things not seen." If God wanted to, He could simply make a grand entrance and prove to the nations that He exists, but that would take away the need for faith.

Witness the birth of a child, the awesome power of Niagara Falls, or the melodic flight of a tiny bumblebee and tell me in your heart of hearts you think all this happened as the result of some Darwinian scientific event? I just can't see it that way. I have seen firsthand the *agape* love of God and how he miraculously lifted me, and so many others, up out of the grips of the Devil's clutches. I have heard His voice, I have seen His handiwork, and I have witnessed His healing. Yet, in the end, His existence is simply a matter of faith: not a foolish, blind leap into a big, dark ocean, but a refreshing dip into a safe and lifegiving pool where 90 percent of Earth's neighbors are already being healed.

There's room for more.

Chapter 10

God and Money

As I was starting to come out of my first depression, I found myself in a mega-bookstore asking the sales clerk to point me toward the books on money and finance. I felt if I spent some time reading about my business, perhaps I would get fired up again and know the choices I was making were "right." But, instead, I just got more flustered. What I saw was overwhelming: shelves and shelves of books talking about money and finances. Though there were scores of titles, the saleswoman told me the average shelf life of each book was only twelve months. Each year, hundreds of new books come out to replace those you can buy today. Over the last several decades, thousands of books on the topic have come and gone proving no one has ever published a financial book that truly works or else it would have been mandatory reading.

With the information changing yearly, I thought, "Where should I begin? Which book should I read first?" Turns out, I already had the world's best-selling, most authoritative guide to money and finances and it is still read by billions of people: *The Holy Bible.*

If you thought the Bible was all about *thee* and *thou* and what not to do, you're sadly misinformed. The second most talked about topic in the Bible, including the subject of nearly half the parables, is money and possessions. Money is mentioned in the Bible more than eight hundred times. It's obvious God knew how important money would be to us.

I find it ironic but not surprising that some in the secular world take exception when I combine God and money in my profession. That's because the financial industry as a whole is morally bankrupt and spiritually depleted. If not for the grace of God, I believe that I would have been a card-carrying member of that group. But, after roughly thirty years in and around the financial industry, I know that my profession can seriously impact people's lives in both negative and positive ways, and giving God's truth about finance is always the best advice.

So, here's my first piece of financial wisdom, and it's the number one most important rule to remember: **God owns everything**. Though it may be hard to accept, you must understand that it's all his: your stuff, your house, your car, everything. He just lets us borrow it while we're here on Earth.

I fought this for decades. I fought it hard. Whether you're fiscally well off or financially struggling, it's a hard concept for almost anyone to accept. *You* may have bought that car or house, but *He* gave you the money to buy it, so it's His. Everything is. Nothing belongs to us, not even ourselves. God owns everything. And I mean everything. You, me, and all that we think and possess. In fact, that which we possess is really only that which God wants us to possess. He can take it all away from us at His will and we will have no control. We are merely stewards or caretakers of His stuff.

Here's the biblical proof:

> The Earth is the Lord's, and everything in it, the world, and all who live in it.—Psalms 24:1

That means that every itty bitty inch of this Earth is His.

> The land is mine and you are but aliens and my tenants. —Leviticus 25:23

We are renters on God's Earth.

> "The silver is mine and the gold is mine," declares the Lord Almighty.—Haggai 2:8

God owns a whole lot more than just silver and gold, but in the context of biblical times, silver and gold were the currency. If the Bible were written today perhaps it would say, "The money, stocks, bonds, securities, real estate, 401(k)s, and pension plans are all mine."

> Remember the Lord your God, for it is He who gives you the ability to produce wealth. —Deuteronomy 8:18

Were it not for the Lord, we wouldn't even have the capacity to earn a living. Wealth is not bad, actually it's good when it comes from God. Where we mess up is when we forget that wealth and everything else come from Him.

> For from him and through him and to him are all things...—Romans 11:36

God not only *owns* everything, he also directs the comings and goings of the world's economy.

> Now it is required that those who have been given a trust must prove faithful.—1 Corinthians 4:2

If you've been given wealth, God wants you to prove your faithfulness with it. Show you are trustworthy with the small stuff and He'll entrust you with the big stuff.

I first realized that we were only stewards of God's property when I read Jesus' story about a wealthy master who went away on a long journey. In his absence, three of his servants were assigned stewardship over his financial affairs. Each servant was given a level of responsibility consistent with his ability. When the master returned, he asked for an accounting of their stewardship, just like we will be asked by our Lord. The first steward was given five talents, or coins. He invested and multiplied the coins and produced five more. He was commended for being a good and faithful servant. The master told him that, since he was faithful with a few things, he shall be in charge of many things.

The second steward, who was given only two coins, produced two more. He, too, was commended for being faithful with little and told he would be given more because of it. The third steward, who was given only one coin, chose to bury it and upon the master's return, eagerly showed him how he managed to hold on to just it. The master became angry and called him wicked and lazy. The master had him tossed outside into the darkness where there will be weeping and gnashing of teeth.

Society has created classes in general and with wealth in particular. I believe that Jesus told this story to make us aware that not only whatever money we have during our mortal lives is His, but it is our duty to invest it wisely. (Keep in mind that the Bible uses stories such as these called parables to teach us.)

Once you realize that what is yours is God's and what's God's is God's, then you will need to use the money that He gives you to build His Kingdom. In the Bible, God calls us all to be "cheerful givers." But in all honesty, could you cheerfully give until it hurts? Jesus spent a lot of time teaching and talking about how getting caught up in money and possessions will eventually hurt us.

In Mark 10:21, we read the story of the rich man who asked what he must do to inherit eternal life. "Jesus looked at him and loved him. 'One thing you lack,' he said. 'Go, sell everything you have and give to the poor, and you will have treasure in heaven. Then come, follow me.'" We are told that the rich man left sadly—he chose his possessions over heavenly treasure. Though Jesus doesn't expect us all to sell everything and become Mother Theresa, we can learn from her. Like Mother Theresa, God wants us to have the heart to do it if called.

In I Timothy 6:6–7 and 17–19 the Bible says, "But godliness with contentment is great gain. For we brought nothing into the world, and we can take nothing out of it.... Command those who are rich in this present world not to be arrogant nor to put their hope in wealth, which is so uncertain, but to put their hope in God, who richly provides us with everything for our enjoyment. Command them to do good, to be rich in good deeds, and to be generous and willing to share. In this way they will lay up treasure for themselves as a firm foundation for the coming age, so that they may take hold of the life that is truly life."

I have long joked that I want to write a book for Catholics and their church giving titled, "One Hundred Ways to Fold a Dollar Bill." For some, perhaps, a dollar is a big gift, but for the vast majority of us, we don't give anywhere near what God calls us to do. Here's what He says in the Bible:

> Will a man rob God? Yet you rob me. But you ask, 'How do we rob you?' In tithes and offerings. You are under a curse—the whole nation of you—because you are robbing me. Bring the whole tithe into the storehouse, that there may be food in my house. Test me in this,' says the Lord Almighty, 'and see if I will not throw open the floodgates of heaven and pour out so much blessing that you will not have room enough for it.'—Malachi 3:8–10

Basically, God is saying that if you do not pay your tithe, a tenth of your earnings, you are robbing Him and putting yourself under a curse. He goes on to say that we should test Him on this and give a full 10 percent, then watch as He opens the floodgates of heaven to pour out His blessings on us—so many blessings that we won't even have room for them all!

> No one can serve two masters. Either he will hate the one and love the other, or he will be devoted to the one and despise the other. You cannot serve both God and Money.—Matthew 6:24

I found this out the hard way, twice. As soon as I was making what I thought was really good money, my heart spent far more time on me and making more money than on God. Our hearts must be devoted to God and not money or we will eventually suffer.

> Do not store up for yourselves treasures on earth, where

moth and rust destroy, and where thieves break in and steal. But store up for yourselves treasures in heaven, where moth and rust do not destroy, and where thieves do not break in and steal. For where your treasure is, there your heart will be also.—Matthew 6:19–21

In this passage of scripture, God is saying that it's a waste to try to accumulate treasure here on Earth, but far better to accumulate treasures in heaven because *where your treasure is, there your heart will be also*. In other words, what you put your effort into is where your heart, your allegiance, and your love will be.

You may have noticed by now that nowhere have I said that money is bad. It's not.

Money itself is a useful tool that should not be deemed evil. It is neither good nor evil. It's merely a medium of exchange; a necessity for basic living. It doesn't cause misuse or abuse—we do!

I believe perhaps the most *mis*quoted verse in the Bible has to be 1 Timothy 6:10—"The love of money is a root of all kinds of evil." Most people erroneously say that *money* is the root of all evil, but as you can see, money is not the problem; it's the *love* of money that's to blame.

I have also made no mention of God using money against us because He doesn't. Just as important as how God uses money to help us, I believe that there are areas God does not use money to influence our lives:

- God never uses money to cause us to worry, suffer anxiety, get us upset, or punish us. There was a time in my life when I would wager a few dollars—okay several dollars. And when I lost money, I would think God was punishing me for gambling. That's nonsense!

• God never uses money to corrupt us. Greed, ego, deceit, and other worldly snares are at odds with God and His plan.

~~~

Accumulating more stuff. It could be an Olympic sport! Keeping up with the Joneses has become a national obsession in the United States and has led us down an unsustainable economic environment of having much but actually "owning" very little of it. Yes, it's okay to want a better house *but with that must come more giving*. The Bible teaches us that in the following verses:

Now he who supplies seed to the sower and bread for food will also supply and increase your store of seed and will enlarge the harvest of your righteousness. You will be made rich in every way so that you can be generous on every occasion, and through us your generosity will result in thanksgiving to God.—II Corinthians 9:10–11

John answered, "The man with two tunics should share with him who has none, and the one who has food should do the same."—Luke 3:11

[T]he Lord Jesus himself said: "It is more blessed to give than to receive."—Acts 20:35

All the believers were one in heart and mind. No one claimed that any of his possessions was his own, but they shared everything they had. There were no needy persons among them. For from time to time those who owned lands or houses sold them, brought the money from the sales and put it at the apostles' feet, and it was distributed to anyone as he had need.—Acts 4:32 and 34–35

What good is it, my brothers, if a man claims to have faith but has no deeds? Can such faith save him? Suppose a brother or sister is without clothes and daily food. If one of you says to him, "Go, I wish you well; keep warm and well fed," but does nothing about his physical needs, what good is it? In the same way, faith by itself, if it is not accompanied by action, is dead.—James 2:14–17

Billionaire publisher Malcom Forbes is credited with saying, "Whoever dies with the most toys wins." Sadly, many of us try to live Forbes' motto of accumulating possessions because we believe the "stuff" will bring us joy. But in the game of life, the winners are not judged by their bank balance. The winners of this game follow His commands, give to His causes, and care for their children and grandchildren and the children of others.

I find it interesting that the meanest life, the poorest existence,is attributed to God's will, but as human beings become more affluent, as their living standard and style begin to ascend the material scale,God descends the scale of responsibility at a commensurate speed.

—Maya Angelou

Proverbs 13:22 says, "A good man leaves an inheritance to his children's children," indicating that God wants us to make a difference, financially, in our family tree.

In case you were wondering where God stands on debt, just read this one simple verse, Proverbs 22:7: "The rich rule over the poor, and the borrower is servant to the lender."

Shakespeare stated it most eloquently in *Hamlet* when he wrote:

> Neither a borrower nor a lender be;
> For loan oft loses both itself and friend,
> And borrowing dulls the edge of husbandry.
> *(Husbandry refers to the careful and thrifty management of affairs and resources.)*

If you haven't made God your number one financial advisor, know for certain that He has much better things in store for you when you do.

Chapter 11

What's Wrong With "Prosperity Christianity"?

As I said in the last chapter, I don't believe we are all called to be Mother Theresa. We're not required to give up every earthly belonging and live in poverty. As a matter of fact, we need to make money and give a good amount of it to the Church, ministries, and charities so we can support the evangelical efforts Christ calls us to do. We know that for three years Jesus's ministry was supported by donations. It wasn't every day that He turned a few loaves and fishes into enough food to feed the masses. No, Jesus used someone else's money to further his ministry, so I am certainly not against raising money to do His work.

As I see it, the problem arises when Church leaders conduct what becomes like a weekly telethon pleading and convincing people to give, and then returning few of those gifts, proportionate to what is collected, to His work. Sadly, those church leaders often live far, far beyond their means on the backs of their flocks. Many of these preachers espouse what is called "Prosperity Theology."

"Prosperity Theology" or "Prosperity Gospel" is the teaching that wealth is a divine reward for one's faith in God and emphasizes God's promised generosity for those believers who claim it. The doctrine holds that material prosperity—financial prosperity as well as success in business and personal life—should be *expected* as evidence of God's favor.

Though the concept of Prosperity Gospel started in the early 1900s, it gained momentum in the 1980s with the help of "televangelists" and has since moved into mainstream Christianity. According to a 2006 *TIME* poll, 17 percent of Christians surveyed said they considered themselves part of such a movement, while a full 61 percent believed that God wants people to be prosperous. The survey also stated that nearly one third agreed that if you give your money to God, God will bless you with more money.

A September 2006 *TIME* article titled, "Does God want you to be rich?"said,

> In a nutshell, it [Prosperity Theology] suggests that a God who loves you does not want you to be broke. Its signature verse could be John 10:10: "I have come that they may have life, and that they may have it more abundantly."

So what's wrong with thinking that God loves you and wants you to prosper? In my opinion, nothing. The Bible tells us that our Heavenly Father loves us, and what father among us would not want the best for his children? But nowhere in the scriptures do I find that we should pray for a BMW and a six-bedroom estate and they just show up simply because we believe. There's nothing wrong with owning a Beemer, mind you, but if you have the money to buy a $75,000 car and multimillion-dollar home, I believe you need to have already sewn hundreds of thousands of dollars and even more in sweat equity into Jesus' work of blessing the meek, the poor, and the unwanted. *The more money you have, the greater the percentage you should be selflessly giving.* Those blessed with financial wealth have a much higher calling to help those who don't. Luke 12:48 tells us that to whom much is given, much is required.

Furthermore, there is biblical evidence for being financially secure here on earth, and that is to care for one's family. The Bible tells us that it is admirable to leave an inheritance even to our grandchildren.

> A good [man] leaveth an inheritance to his children's children: and the wealth of the sinner [is] laid up for the just.—Proverbs 13:22

Yet, I believe prosperity preachers spend too much time emphasizing accumulating material things, and far less time on His work. It's materialism masquerading as theology. Here are a few scriptures to help you understand why I think placing such emphasis on prosperity and gaining wealth is really false teaching:

> For we brought nothing into this world, and it is certain we can carry nothing out. And having food and clothing, with these we shall be content. But those who desire to be rich fall into temptation and a snare, and into many foolish and harmful lusts which drown men in destruction and perdition. For the love of money is a root of all kinds of evil, for which some have strayed from the faith in their greediness, and pierced themselves through with many sorrows.—I Timothy 6:7–10

> Do not store up for yourselves treasures on earth, where moth and rust consume, and where thieves break in and

steal, but store up for yourselves treasures in heaven. . . . For where your treasure is, there your heart will be also. No one can serve two masters. Either he will hate the one and love the other, or he will be devoted to the one and despise the other. You cannot serve both God and Money.—Matthew 6:19–21, 24; Luke 16:13

Do not love the world or the things in the world. If anyone loves the world, the love of the Father is not in him.—I John 2:15

If anyone teaches false doctrines and does not agree to the sound instruction of our Lord Jesus Christ and to godly teaching, he is conceited and understands nothing. He has an unhealthy interest in controversies and quarrels about words that result in envy, strife, malicious talk, evil suspicions, and constant friction between men of corrupt mind, who have been robbed of the truth and who think that godliness is a means to financial gain.
—I Timothy 6:3–5

Jesus said to him, "If you wish to be complete, go and sell your possessions and give to the poor, and you will have treasure in heaven; and come, follow Me."
—Matthew 19:21

Mega-church Pastor Rick Warren, *New York Times* best-selling author of *The Purpose Driven Life* and a noted critic of the prosperity churches, is quoted as saying, "I don't think it is a sin to be rich, it's a sin to die rich. I want people to make as much money as they can as long as they give it away as much as they can." I couldn't have said it better. Warren went on to add, "This idea that God wants everyone to be wealthy? There is a word for that: baloney."

Like Warren, I believe this heresy is a form of idolatry. You can't measure your self worth by your net worth. There are millions of faithful followers of Christ who live in poverty, and if God wants us all to be rich, why isn't everyone in the Church a millionaire?

Please note that I am not suggesting that every priest, preacher, or pastor who has appeared on TV is up to no good. As a matter of fact, I have heard no one more prophetic than Charles Stanley who has a massive TV- and Internet-based ministry. But Stanley's preaching is far more about educating people about the scriptures and the love of Christ than it is about prosperity. He has helped me understand faith at a much higher level.

I struggle with the lifestyles of many of the prosperity televangelist pastors, and believe they spend little time "carrying the cross." By and large, their messages appeal to those whose knowledge of scripture is minimal, and instead call out to their vanity and desire for wealth and success. I also believe their well-staged and slickly produced "shows," which are more entertainment than real preaching, take advantage of the poor and working middle class, especially when the economy is not doing well. It becomes like a lottery ticket as these folks sow what little they have, but it is the Church that does most of the reaping.

As their followers watch from their modest homes, condos, and apartment buildings, these televangelist prosperity preachers go home to $10 million estates. In my opinion, a $1 million or $2 million home should be comfortable enough, and the other $8 million or $9 million could help a lot of people. Similarly, do TV evangelists need private jets to carry out God's work? Wouldn't flying first class be adequately comfortable, leaving a lot of extra money to feed and clothe the poor?

Remember, I don't believe Jesus is against money, He just wants us to use it well and for His work, not our own glorification. Throughout the Gospels, we find Jesus urging those blessed with wealth to give a significant portion to the less fortunate. As shown in the earlier scripture references, He speaks often about how chasing wealth is not godly and is dangerous to your eternal salvation.

Perhaps the most interesting scripture one could use to judge the prosperity preachers is this:

> Unlike so many, we do not peddle the word of God for profit. On the contrary, in Christ we speak before God with sincerity, like men sent from God.
> —II Corinthians 2:17

We read in II Peter about a "false teacher" who came in the name of Jesus Christ:

> But there were false prophets among the people, even as there will be false teachers among you, who will secretly bring in destructive heresies, even denying the Lord who bought them, and bring on themselves swift destruction. And many will follow their destructive ways, because of whom the way of truth will be blasphemed. By covetousness they will exploit you with deceptive words; for a long time their judgment has not been idle, and their destruction does not slumber.—II Peter 2:1–3

The New International Version (NIV) reads the first part of II Peter 2:3 as:

> In their greed these teachers will exploit you with stories they have made up...

The NIV Study Bible note says:

> In their greed: They will be motivated by a desire for money and will commercialize the Christian faith to their own selfish advantage.

In total contrast to the claims of the prosperity-preaching money-men, the Bible tells us not to give money to the wealthy. On the contrary, the Bible says that to give to the rich will lead to poverty.

> He who oppresses the poor to increase his wealth and he who gives gifts to the rich—both come to poverty.
> —Proverbs 22:16

Finally, instead of stressing the importance of wealth, the Bible warns against pursuing it. Believers, particularly leaders in the Church, are to be free from the love of money because the Bible tells us clearly that the love of money is the root of all evil. Remember, the one showing up to preach a false gospel could look like an angel, but that doesn't make his words true—his words will be damned:

> But even if we or an angel from heaven should preach a gospel other than the one we preached to you, let him be eternally condemned! As we have already said, so now I say again: If anybody is preaching to you a gospel other than what you accepted, let him be eternally condemned!—Galatians 1:8–9

The *Bottomline* is this: it's okay to be financially successful—okay with the Bible, okay with God—but wealth is not guaranteed simply because you believe in Christ. Those who do realize financial and material success, however, are called by God to sow their financial rewards into good, Godly works.

In my opinion, that doesn't mean sending a demanding TV preacher $58 because he claims there are 58 blessings in the Bible, or $90 because he promises you'll get a raise in 90 days, or any other such cockamamie scheme, especially when that preacher is living an indulgent, lavish, and sinfully luxurious lifestyle thanks to your donations.

Chapter 12

What Three Decades In and Around Wall Street Have Taught Me About Investing

You've heard the old saying, if I only knew then what I know now? How true that really is. When I think of how I was promoted to head of investment strategy in 1987 with less than three years' experience, I wonder how I managed. I spent most of my energies buying and selling stocks and foolishly believing I could continuously predict what the stock market would do, and I spent little time on learning and appreciating how money really works. It was not until I met Frank Congilose in 1998 that I was shown the real truth about money and that traditional financial planning, a process 98 percent of all investors employ (and one which is steered by "professional advisors"), is a horribly flawed process.

Back in the eighties, most professionals used a simple legal pad to show clients how to set up their "financial plans." Nowadays, firms use fancy computer applications with all sorts of interactive charts and graphs. But in the end, whether on a legal pad or high-tech computer model, all of these "plans" do the same thing: They guess.

First, they seek a dollar number the client believes (or is shown) he or she will need to live happily ever after. This is the first absolute *guess*. Once that is agreed upon, the professional advisor picks a product or products—most involve stocks, mutual funds, etc.—and, based on past performance, projects similar returns for the future in order to reach that magical happily-ever-after figure. This is the second raw *guess*—a total shot in the dark as to how high or low future returns will be.

What's wrong with this very unscientific method? Four economic factors have a major impact on any financial plan, and unless you have a crystal ball you're simply guessing where they'll be at any given time. They are:

1. Interest rates
2. Tax rates
3. Inflation rates
4. Rates of return

I'm going to let you in on a little secret: I can't accurately predict the course of all four of these *and neither can anyone else* except Almighty God. Therefore, despite the average plan having hypothetical assumptions of these four factors, one or more of them will not be accurately assumed. One could get lucky as some did in the 1990s when everything was doing well, but do you want to depend on good fortune to keep your fortune? This is simply a well-established guessing game with all the bells and whistles. Make no mistake about it: traditional financial planning is a guessing game—a high-stakes round of hangman, charades, or twenty questions.

I don't know about you, but I don't want to leave my family's security to chance. That's why I was so awestruck by the process Frank Congilose introduced to me; one that employs the two most important money facts:

1.   Lost opportunity cost
2.   Velocity of money

Let me explain: If you had $20 and lost it, how much did you lose? Twenty dollars, right? Wrong. You lost the $20 *plus* whatever that twenty bucks could have earned if you had it. That is a lost opportunity cost (LOC). Just about everyone and every business has LOCs. The key to financial success is identifying the LOCs and putting them back on the right side of the ledger—your side!

If you were to identify about $20 a week (a few cups of latte, perhaps?) you could save, that would add up to $1,000 a year in savings. But it's so much more when you take into consideration the LOCs. By saving that $1,000 per year, over twenty-five years you would save $25,000 plus the lost earnings on that money of over $18,000 (that's at the modest interest rate of only 4 percent) for a total LOC of over $43,000. At 5 percent interest, the number increases to over $50,000. That $50K becomes part of your cash flow.

Cash flow, in case you didn't know, is nothing more than the money that comes in and the money that goes out. If you spend more than you make you have a *negative* cash flow. If you make more than you spend (leaving some extra) you have a *positive* cash flow. Obviously, increasing the positive cash flow allows you to save more and accumulate more wealth.

No one knows more about money and cash flow than banks. They don't produce anything yet they are able to turn one dollar into two or three or more. Here's how it works: you deposit a dollar in the bank. The bank pays you interest on that dollar. The bank then lends your dollar out to someone else at a higher rate. How much higher depends on what type of loan the borrower takes. Not only is the rate they charge higher than they paid you, but they get to lend your dollar out two or three times on average. During the time your dollar is deposited in the bank, it may be loaned out for a car loan, personal loan, home equity loan, mortgage, or credit card. Each time the bank loans out your dollar they make money by way of charging the borrower more interest than they are paying you.

This is called the velocity of money, the average rate at which money is exchanged from one transaction to another. Velocity is the frequency with which a unit of money is spent over a specific time period. The bank has taken full advantage of the velocity of money and effectively made a dollar do the work of two or three or more. What I learned to do through the services of Frank and his associates is help people understand and take advantage of the velocity of money in their own finances just like banks do.

Another way to appreciate velocity of money is to take a penny and double it once a day. On day one you double a penny and end up with two cents. On day two you double your two cents and have four. On day three you double your four cents and have eight ... and so on. How long before you have over a million dollars? It may shock you, but it's only twenty-seven days. That's right: a penny doubled each day for twenty-seven days is worth $1,342,177.20.

Without any out-of-pocket expenses or substantial risk, you can add hundreds of thousands of dollars to your worth over a lifetime by simply capturing LOCs and employing velocity of money strategies, which in turn increase cash flow. The sooner you learn that the key to successful finances is cash flow (saving your money instead of trying to gamble on an asset's appreciation in price to increase net worth), the better off you will be.

<u>Four Approaches to Money Matters:</u>

I have found that there are four basic ways most people approach money matters. In which group do you fall?

1. The "No Planning" Approach
This is the person with absolutely no plan. Nothing. Nada. Wing and a prayer. Their entire plan is to worry about it tomorrow. Obviously, this is the worst-case scenario.

2. The "Occasional Planning" Approach
This is the person who intermittently thinks about money matters and might put forth a halfhearted attempt at a plan, especially right after New Year's, but soon the day-to-day grind of life takes over and they end up doing what the no planning group does; worry about it starting tomorrow. But tomorrow never comes.

3. The "Needs Planning" Approach
This is the person who plans for specific events like college or a child's wedding but does not have an overall, integrated financial plan. They at times actually progress on a specific goal only to find out they have let other important goals fall by the wayside and then try to catch up with some "Hail Mary" schemes.

4. The True "Financial Planning" Approach
The infrequent person who seriously plans for the things life throws at us. Not just retirement, mind you, but life. Buying a home, taking vacations, saving for college and

retirement, and a nest egg for those things that just crop up.

Even among those who do plan, there are speed bumps along the way. In my three decades on Wall Street, I have seen many of the same mistakes time and time again. Here, I have assembled my list of Top Ten Biggest Investment Mistakes.

Peter Grandich's
Top Ten Biggest Investment Mistakes:

10. "Hot Potato" buying—Buying the popular stocks of the day or the latest get-rich-quick scheme. Unless you have a crooked rabbit, the turtle always wins this race in investing.

9. Believing publications—You see it all the time. Some magazine headline that reads "Ten sure-fire ways to riches," or "Ten stocks to beat the market," etc., all for the low, low price of a few bucks for that issue. While there are some really useful publications, magazines like *Money* who depend mostly on financial institutions for advertisement are, in my opinion, always tilted to the cup being half full and are not truly objective.

8. Failing to consider spouse's views—Guilty as charged. Through my first making of millions, then losing a good portion of it, my wife's only regret was I didn't take into account her desires and wishes. Family financial planning must be a team effort.

7. Believing money is evil—Yes, the love of money is evil, but money itself is not. It's a necessity but not to the point where we literally lose our eternal life with the true owner of it. Some people are afraid of it and what owning a hefty sum of it may do to them. As stated earlier, if you truly come to understand you're only a steward with it, you are likely to do much good with it.

6. Not fully understanding what you're doing—The less you know, the more people who live off the less knowledgeable can thrive. God knew how important matters of money would be and dedicated a good portion of His life's manual (the Bible) to it. Shouldn't you make a similar effort?

5. Inability to judge worthiness of risk—Here's a news flash: if it's too good to be true, it's too good to be true. If the banks are paying you 1 percent and someone says you can make 10 percent, you better know that there's a certain degree of risk that comes with the potential. Many times the anguish of a loss far outweighs the dollar amount, and it lasts longer and impacts other areas of your life.

4. Trusting financial institutions—Despite decades of deceit and fraud throughout the financial industry, most people still place a large degree of blind trust in the financial institutions and the personnel with whom they deal. Any financial adviser worth his or her weight should have a well-documented and long track record of success or at least have numerous references. Wouldn't you be glad to give a reference if your adviser did well for you? Run, don't walk, from those who can't provide them.

3. "Hope" is not an investment strategy—When it comes to faith, hope is very good, but in investing it can be a killer. If I only had a dollar for every time I heard an investor say they're "hoping" their stock goes back up so they can get their money back. Look, if you're hoping the price will rise yet not willing to buy more at the reduced price, who do you expect to do so and pay up to the price you originally paid? Just hoping for these changes without sound fundamental reasons to back up that hope is a license for disaster.

2. No written financial strategy at all—Similar to the "No Planning" approach. Like anything else at which you want to succeed, you must write it down. In the landmark book *The Magic of Thinking Big*, author David J. Schwartz tells us to write down our goals—all of them. Financial goals are no different. Writing your plan down not only keeps you on track but acts as a benchmark as you achieve your financial goals. One of the first things to do is to take a thirty-day account of every dime you spend—and I mean everything. Almost always, people are surprised how much they spend and on what. They soon realize they can either do without some things or spend less on them.

And the number one biggest investment mistake is...

1. Procrastination—Without a doubt, putting off dealing with matters of finance is the single biggest investment mistake. Whether it's by accident or on purpose, delaying dealing with finances can only hurt.

~~~

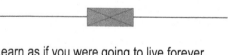

Learn as if you were going to live forever.
Live as if you were going to die tomorrow.

—Mahatma Gandhi

Perhaps we can all take some advice from one of the richest men ever to walk this earth. No, not Donald Trump or Warren Buffet, but King Solomon.

He was one of the Bible's best investors. King Solomon has a fantastic track record based on three basic biblical principles:

Principle #1—Diversification

> Divide your portion to seven, or even to eight, for you do not know what misfortune may occur on the earth.
> —Ecclesiastes 11:2

King Solomon knew that you don't put all your eggs in one basket. This is especially true for those people who put all of their 401(k) savings into their company's stock.

Principle #2 - Good Counsel

> Without consultation, plans are frustrated, but with many counselors they succeed.—Proverbs 15:22

There's no one person who can give universal counsel. Not only do you need to develop a support team, but you need to find a diverse group of a few individuals because one team member is not always aware of what another is doing and having someone quarterback all the different team players is important.

Principle #3—Ethical Investing

> The conclusion, when all has been heard, is fear God and keep His commandments.—Ecclesiastes 12:13

Not only should we be honest in our investments but make sure where we place our monies to be Godly. That's different for every individual, but might include avoiding investing in businesses involved in alcohol, weapons, tobacco, or companies with questionable human rights practices.

Remember this: on Wall Street there are bulls, bears, and pigs. The bulls and bears each have their day, but the pigs always end up at the slaughterhouse.

Chapter 13

Retirement:
A Man-Made Myth

*"Retirement at 65 is ridiculous.
When I was 65, I still had pimples."*
~ George Burns

There are a lot of things I can point to as being wrong with our society today, but one glaringly obvious shortfall is our entitlement mentality. In general, we feel we "deserve" a whole lot of stuff that we really have no right to claim. First and foremost, in my opinion, is the concept of retirement.

Make no mistake about it: this whole notion of retirement is a man-made creation. There's nothing biblical about us supposedly killing ourselves for 75 percent of our years to store up enough assets to live off for the last 25 percent, yet that's the system our society has built. The system is hopelessly broken and our government can do little more than try once again to kick the can down to the next generation. Somebody is going to pay an awful price.

Let me give you a little background on the phenomenon we call "retirement."

In her *New York Times* article titled "The History of Retirement, From Early Man to A.A.R.P.", author Mary-Lou Weisman briefly and humorously outlines the history of retirement from Cave Man to modern day, and gives supporting facts about why retirement is not just man-made, but a twentieth-century creation.

During the Stone Age, says Weisman, we worked until age twenty then died, usually from unnatural causes. During biblical times, when people lived to be *really* old—the Bible says Methuselah died at the ripe old age of 969, thus the adage "older than Methuselah"—people worked until they dropped.

This working-until-your-last-breath mentality prevailed through the centuries even after Chancellor Otto Von Bismarck, nicknamed The Iron Chancellor, introduced the concept of retirement. In 1889, Germany's Old Age Disability Insurance Bill was enacted to provide a pension for all workers at age sixty-five. Sounds generous? Not really. It was proposed by Bismarck as a way of gaining favor among his countrymen, but it wasn't as sweet a deal as you might think. The average life expectancy at the time was forty-five, so there weren't many around at sixty-five to collect, and those who did usually didn't live a whole lot longer.

What Bismarck's bill did, however, was put in motion the idea that at some point in life we deserve to plop down in our rocking chair and grow mold. Did I say mold? I meant old. As Weisman describes, that single move "set the arbitrary world standard for the exact year at which old age begins and established the precedent that government should pay people for growing old."

Fast forward to 1905 when world-renowned physician William Osler, in his valedictory address at the Johns Hopkins Hospital, where he had been physician-in-chief, said that workers aged forty to sixty were less productive than their younger counterparts and those over age sixty were "useless" on average. That must have been popular. At the time, around 60 percent of men aged sixty-five and older were still in the workforce.

But it wasn't until President Franklin D. Roosevelt signed the Social Security Act of 1935, also known as the federal old-age program, that retirement and entitlements, which were mostly available only to white men, became a part of American culture. The average life expectancy in America was just under sixty-two years. Roosevelt's old-age program was funded by a 1 percent tax on employers and employees on the first $3,000 of a worker's earnings. Today, the Social Security tax rate is more than 6 percent.

The end result of the retirement revolution? The number of working men age sixty-five and older dropped from around 78 percent in 1880 to less than 20 percent in 1990. When you figure in the increased life expectancy over that hundred-year period, it's clear that we spend a much larger part of our lives *not working* than our forefathers could ever have dreamed. In 2010, nearly 53 million Americans collected Social Security to the tune of $703 billion.

"The retirement pattern we see today, typically involving decades of self-financed leisure, developed gradually over the last century," says Joanna Short, professor of economics at Augustana College, Illinois, in the article "Economic History of Retirement in the United States."

"Economic historians have shown that rising labor market and pension income largely explain the dramatic rise of retirement. Rather than being pushed out of the labor force because of increasing obsolescence, older men have increasingly chosen to use their rising income to finance an earlier exit from the labor force." [Note: she refers only to men because historical data is not available on women.]

Why is this important?

In 2009, I moved into an adult community. Between what I have seen here and what I see in the news, I'm left wondering what happened to the "Golden Years." The "Don't Worry, Be Happy" crowd on Wall Street had for years touted the great wealth transfer (which was to occur when the Baby Boomers started cashing in their savings) as a source of big business for them for years to come. They knew most investors bought into the myth that stocks and home prices would just keep going up over time. They built all sorts of products in hopes of catching the inevitable transfer of wealth from one generation to another but somehow missed seeing a financial crisis that they would like to tout is over. In my opinion, however, the worst is yet to come.

So, seniors found themselves unable to secure high-yielding, safe investments and their prime assets like their homes and stock portfolios no longer simply rose in value over time. This would be bad enough but the last factor that up until now gave seniors critical comfort, affordable and high-quality medical care via Medicare, is about to go the way of the first two. The inability to access the top-notch medical care that this generation has grown accustomed to will not only be the dagger that ends the Golden Years, but perhaps give seniors the biggest cause for fears.

There are other factors that, when combined with the above, make for some social, political, and economical episodes that aren't going to be pretty. Keep in mind that it was just a few years ago when, for the first time in American history, we had more Americans over the age of sixty-five than under eighteen. About 80 percent of the wealth in America is owned by empty-nesters and seniors who also tend to vote more than younger Americans, and in their own interest.

Don't assume, as the financial industry did, that snow on the roof means dough in the pocket. A recent survey conducted by CESI Debt Solutions discovered that 56 percent of American retirees still had outstanding debts when they retired. Retirement is not supposed to be about debt. In fact, it is hard enough to try to survive on a fixed income without having to worry about debt payments. But now the majority of Americans who retire do so with debt still on the books.

A September 7, 2011, *Wall Street Journal* article by E. S. Browning entitled "Debt Hobbles Older Americans" put it like this:

> More Americans are reaching their 60s with so much debt they can't afford to retire.
>
> Most people used to pay off their debts before retiring. But as wages have barely kept up with rising prices over the past 35 years Americans have pushed debt higher, living beyond their means. Now, people are postponing retirement, cutting living standards or both.

Worse yet is that an increasing number of senior citizens are going bankrupt. A University of Michigan study found that Americans who are fifty-five years of age or older now account for 20 percent of all the bankruptcies in the United

States. Back in 2001, they only accounted for 12 percent of bankruptcies. In fact, between 1991 and 2007, the number of Americans between the ages of sixty-five and seventy-four who filed for bankruptcy rose by a staggering 178 percent.

Needless to say, many elderly Americans are under such financial stress that they have simply decided never to retire. According to a recent AARP survey of Baby Boomers, 40 percent of them plan to work "until they drop." Not because they want to. Because they have to.

Another study, titled "The Impact of Deferring Retirement Age on Retirement Income Adequacy" conducted by the Employee Benefit Research Institute, shows almost all Americans will have to work longer than they had anticipated. Released in June 2011, the study says that most in the US will have to keep working well into their seventies and eighties to afford retirement.

Does that mean we are coming back around to the times of Otto Von Bismarck when all men died with their boots on? Perhaps.

Trust me, I am not the only one pondering all this. An April 2011 Gallup poll showed that 66 percent of Americans are very or moderately worried about not having enough money for retirement. Retirement worries have topped the charts in the annual survey on the economy and personal finance since the early 2000s, but the percentage of people who are very worried about it is significantly higher since 2008. Even the younger crowd is worked up over funding retirement. Seventy-seven percent of Americans aged thirty to forty-nine are very or somewhat worried. In all, the poll says roughly two-thirds of all Americans at all income levels are worried about not having enough money for retirement.

And, then there is the inflation worry.

"Inflation," you ask? "Of all things, you warn us about inflation?"

Absolutely. Journalist Robert Powell said it best in a March 7, 2011 *Marketwatch* article, when he called inflation "one of the most insidious risks Americans will face in retirement." He goes on to say that even though those nearing retirement have witnessed firsthand the devastating adverse effects of inflation (remember when gas was a buck a gallon?), they just aren't factoring inflation into retirement plans. Research published by the Society of Actuaries says, "Compared to other planning activities, only 72 percent of pre-retirees and 55 percent of retirees are calculating the effects of inflation on their retirement planning."

Why is inflation such a big deal? Because though it only sounds like a few bucks, when compounded over many years, inflation adds up to a financial nightmare from which you won't be able to wake.

Here's an example: if inflation rises at a rate of 3 percent on average, in just ten years you'll need 30 percent more money to buy the exact same thing. A $10 item will cost $13 simply because of inflation. Put a few zeros on the end and it becomes even more apparent: a $30,000 car will cost $39,000. And it you're planning on living for twenty years after retirement, that same hypothetical car is estimated to cost 80 percent more or a whopping $54,000 just because of inflation.

Who among us has anticipates needing 80 percent more money to buy the same goods and services? Those still working will likely see wage increases over the years to keep up with inflation, but the retired likely will not. Though you can try your best to invest in assets that protect your purchasing power, there's no crystal ball. So, the challenge in retirement has become how to spend time without spending money.

My advice?

If you're at or approaching retirement age, don't feel like you're entitled to stop working. Nowhere is it written in the Bible, the Magna Carta, Declaration of Independence, Bill of Rights, Emancipation Proclamation, or any other critical document of knowledge and freedom that "Upon one's sixty-sixth birthday, ye shall lay down your shovel and relax." That isn't how God intended it. It isn't even how Otto Von Bismarck intended it. The United States Centers for Disease Control and Prevention estimate the average life expectancy in America to be just under seventy-eight years. If you retire at sixty-five, what exactly will you do for the next decade or so? And then what will you leave to your kids?

A good man leaves an inheritance for his children's children.—Proverbs 13:22

Here's the *Bottomline*:

For years I've stated that Wall Street and Madison Avenue have knowingly or unknowingly conspired to create a false premise that more money will equal more happiness. They would like you to believe that a bus driver can never be happier than the guy who owns the bus company. Their typical advertisements show "happy people" doing the things the world says "makes you happy." They especially prey on the elderly and suggest that their services will render your Golden Years carefree, enabling you to live a life you couldn't afford when you were working full time. The reality, in my opinion, is that for the most part only the people selling the products and services will be carefree.

As a Christian, I'm especially troubled that our focus on wealth accumulation in order to secure a happy retirement is not only mentally and physically life-threatening, as people literally kill themselves trying to make enough to retire, but a slap in our Creator's face that trusting in Him is not enough. The Forbes maxim "He who dies with the most toys wins" is really a ploy by the evil one to get us to think "things" will give us fullness and contentment. If that was the case, why are so many Hollywood stars and professional athletes so messed up despite making salaries unheard of to most common folk?

There's no biblical verse I know of that suggests God wants us to spend our life doing as little as possible between here and Florida in the winter. I am not suggesting you don't have a financial strategy in place to fund your golden years, because the fact is some of us will not be healthy enough to keep working even if we wanted to. So do your best to plan and save and invest as King Solomon did. Save, watch your LOCs, and employ the velocity of money. And, if in your twilight years you have been blessed with wealth and do not have to work a job, I truly believe those years should be used not as a staging area for our next life but to help those less fortunate. Giving, doing, and volunteering for the causes that help the sick, poor, and disenfranchised is a bare minimum.

Chapter 14

The End of
Grandich Publications

In 2011, when *Confessions of a Wall Street Whiz Kid* was first published, if you had asked me if I envisioned printing any future updates to the book, I would have told you no. Why would there be a need? After having endured years of physical, financial and psychological hell, I was having perhaps the best time of my life. Grandich Publications had so many clients it was a challenge for this one-man band to keep up with all of them. Gold hit record highs of close to $2,000 an ounce. Because of my high-profile forecasts on gold, my wife and daughter joined me on an all-expense paid trip to a sold-out conference in London where I was a keynote speaker, and family members from Ireland and England made the trip to the British capital to visit us there. I got into horse ownership again, this time investing in Standardbreds, and my personal wealth was twice as high as it had been back in 2008 when I had my last bout of heavy turbulence. Little did I know that the dark clouds were on the horizon, but thankfully this time around it appears that I have the proper gear to weather the storm.

As long-time followers know, I have always gone out of my way to tell people to be careful. I have stated again and again that failure is the norm in the junior resource business and that it is one out of a hundred companies that makes it over the long term into a significant company...it's just the nature of this risky business. I said over and over how investing in these types of stocks was highly speculative (and the word speculating was the word Wall Street used so it didn't have to say what it really was – gambling) and one should never invest money you couldn't afford to lose. I would urge—if not plead—with investors that only a small portion of their assets be deployed in this sector. All of this, of course, was absolutely right. The problem is I didn't heed my own advice.

Beginning in late 2011, gold suddenly hit a series of "air pockets" and while it had all the makings of a manipulated sell-off, gold declined through the end of 2013 and took the junior resource market—the backbone of my Grandich Publications clientele—with it. The long list of clients which took years to build up was torn apart in a matter of months. Losing business left and right was bad enough, but my serious error in judgment—owning far too many shares of junior resource stocks—resulted in a whopping 70 percent loss of personal wealth by the end of 2013. I had literally bet the ranch on my clients and was left with nothing more than the dog house I was now in by the time it was over.

But as the saying goes, when God closes a door, He opens a window.

My daughter's Godfather told me recently that he was glad things unfolded as they did because it finally made me get out of a business that was leading to heartache. Though I had known and endlessly warned of overwhelming numbers of failures for the few successes, the fact that my client list eventually faced those same averages led to an ever-increasing physical and financial burden that nearly unraveled the good that had come out of my past "valleys."

As gold and the junior resource market fell, the lack of real solid management at many of these juniors, including my own clients, became glaringly obvious. In more than one case I witnessed truly inept and imprudent management and a total lack of consideration for the very people who had put them in their positions: shareholders. As the drama unfolded and the truth was revealed, I resigned from many clients and today I care little about how some malcontents saw it (and cowardly expressed their twisted views through the anonymity of their keyboards).

But during another "valley" in my walk, I saw God's hands yet again.

As noted earlier in the book, my "other" business, Trinity Financial Sports & Entertainment Management Co., came to life at the beginning of the new millennium. And while it grew in terms of the number of professional athletes associated with it and did a good amount of charitable and spiritual good deeds, it was by no means my main source of income. Grandich Publications put food on my table. But that changed in 2012.

You may recall the story of my association with twin brothers David and John Suckey who both worked for Frank Congilose. Over the past many years, I have spent countless hours with them and consider them to be dear friends. When my daughter was young it was David who was entrusted to watch over her trust should anything happen to me, and now that Tara is grown, David is the trustee for her and Mary. A protégé of my financial mentor, Frank Congilose, David pointed out how Trinity Financial had grown despite me sometimes treating it as a stepchild, and suggested that with our full attention he thought it would flourish.

With gold in the toilet, the junior resource market on life support and me dreading the daily grind, I took him up on his suggestion of hosting a local seminar. The agenda included a discussion of Frank's unique alternative to traditional financial planning strategy and my macroeconomic outlook. We held it locally and invited, among others, readers of Grandich Publications. Among the attendees was a doctor from Maryland who—unbeknownst to me—had been traveling to seminars throughout North America to hear me speak, but this would be the first time we mingled. As a result of that seminar and the trust he had in me, David, Frank and the process they teach—he became not only my single biggest client, but the largest client ever in Frank's 30-year history.

I came to realize that nothing about Grandich Publications could compare to the service I am now able to provide. As a result of that one seminar and the business that followed, this client is now in a remarkably wealthier and safer financial position. Yes, we are compensated for our efforts, but far better than any compensation has been the knowledge that we helped this man and his family safeguard a lifestyle and security that he otherwise may not have obtained. With Grandich Publications, no matter how upfront I was about the risks and likely results, I dealt daily with a barrage of "fan" mail, mental anguish, and physical and emotional stress. The dichotomy could not be more apparent and was like a message from God that now was the time to act. Needless to say, I acted; and now Trinity Financial and a new sports-related venture provide the bulk of my livelihood and bring overflowing joy day in and day out.

146

After clawing my way out of two previous valleys wherein the end of my life was a distinct possibility, this 2013 slump was different. Though it may have brought about a sharp reduction on my balance sheet, my spiritual and mental health have held strong. I attribute this to the fact that I have finally stopped worshipping money, and I now live by Romans 8:28 versus just quoting it: "And we know that in all things God works for the good of those who love him, who have been called according to his purpose."

So as things seemingly got worse and worse in the metals and mining industry in 2013, windows were indeed opening up elsewhere.

While the vast majority of people and organizations I met throughout my life in the metals and mining industry would not measure up, I did meet some very good people. One of them had been interviewing me for years and was in my mind a true conservative and Canada's most listened-to financial radio talk show host, Mr. Michael Campbell. A mere mention of what was unfolding in my life brought on a discussion of potentially writing for his website, more frequent appearances on his radio show and possibly more speaking engagements in Canada.

As God works (all the time!), I met another Canadian after several years of searching.

I mentioned on my blog from time to time about the alternative to traditional financial planning that Dave Suckey and Frank Congilose practice. I stated that while they could help U.S. residents, due to regulatory constraints, they couldn't accept Canadian clients. For years I tried finding someone in Canada like them, but unfortunately, like in the U.S., 99% of so-called financial advisers do it the old fashioned way—they profit more from the advice they give than you do!

God's hands showed up again as I spoke with perhaps one of the toughest Canadian financial journalists. As tough as he was, he and I hit it off, and when I mentioned my plight he suggested I speak with Paul Philip. I did, and my search for a Canadian counterpart was over. What do you think are the chances that Paul would end up being the Canadian protégée of the man who helped teach Frank Congilose many years ago? One-in-a-million if you ask me, but that's God. With Him all things are possible.

By late 2013, I agreed to become Michael Campbell's "Senior Markets Commentator" and I packed up Grandich Publications by shifting all my market commentaries to his website. My involvement with the metals and mining industry has been purposely restricted to just another industry sector I look at in the "whole" market picture.

Words like "coincidence" and "luck" haven't been in my vocabulary for years now. Sayings like "nothing happens for no reason" is branded on my palm to remind me that God is always working in all our lives no matter how unrealistic that may seem at the time. Case in point: While it's apparent by looking at me that I was never intended to be an athlete, for the past several years I have been surrounded by numerous high-profile sports stars. It's a dream come true for the kid from the Bronx. Those associations (which I know have been lined up by the Almighty) led to my newest business venture—the Athletes & Business Alliance (ABA).

By being actively involved with so many current and retired athletes who still have immense popularity, I realized that there weren't opportunities for athletes to meet the members of the business community who may be interested in their skills. Though available through various sports booking agencies, the fees charged make player appearances seem financially out of reach to some businesses. That's why I formed the ABA. This one-of-a-kind Alliance boasts a select membership of diverse senior-level executives, high-net-worth business owners, and both active and retired pro athletes. By invitation only, business execs exchange ideas and build personal relationships with athletes who—by virtue of their celebrity and drive to succeed—are uniquely positioned to help businesses achieve their marketing goals. Though it's a new venture, it's showing great promise...and man, it's a lot of fun!

And God has again allowed my finances to greatly improve despite my best efforts to sabotage them. The Creator of all that is good in the universe continues to give this sinner an abundant life. Praise God.

Chapter 15

Repentance: a New Beginning

"God grant me the serenity to accept
the things I cannot change,
the courage to change the things I can,
and the wisdom to know the difference."
- Reinhold Niebuhr

One of the many challenges for Christians is to decipher what is really discernment from the Holy Spirit and what is the voice of our flawed human nature. For me, that's been especially difficult. But thankfully, the good Lord has sent holy Christian men and women into my life who have helped greatly in this area.

One is Jo Schloeder, the friend and writer who helped me author Confessions. When we met over lunch and I shared with her the tug on my heart to do a third edition, she got it. She had lived through the ups and downs (and ups again) of my life since the new millennium, and she had witnessed firsthand how much of my 31st year in and around Wall Street was spent going through a sort of financial conversion, only to conclude that much of what Wall Street preaches to the masses is flawed, sinful and downright sacrilegious. Jo confirmed my desire to contemplate the things of God, which allows me to get ever closer to the core of my faith.

Another "discerner" for me was George McGovern, New York Metro Area Director and Chapel Coordinator for the New York Football Giants and the New York Yankees, whom I talked about previously. Perhaps no one better understands or has personally witnessed my journey more than George (who is, in my opinion, a near-perfect example of how a Christian man is to live his life). I so appreciate George's friendship, wisdom and Christian example. He was front and center in 2008 when my battle with depression hit me harder than any defensive player he ever knew. And though it was truly touch-and-go for a while, with the help of people like George, I eventually received what God promises us in Romans 8:28, "...all things work together for good to them that love God, to them who are called according to his purpose." Through the many gifts of the Holy Spirit that I have witnessed in George, I have gradually come to see the mission of Peter Grandich clearly ahead of me. It is one that is bringing me closer to God; one that is far away from the "old fashioned" way of Wall Street.

For the past 15 years, my companies have had offices within the headquarters of C & A Financial Group, the business of my financial mentor, Frank Congolise, about whom I wrote in previous chapters. He has come to be another of the people whom I believe God placed in my path to help me distinguish between what is truly God and what is my dumb self. Frank's company helps people live a life of financial balance and fulfillment. They provide a holistic view of a client's financial life through a process that Frank developed and calls the "Responsible Wealth Architect Process." This approach teaches clients how to improve their cash flow now and at retirement so they can enjoy an improved quality of life. Keeping that perspective, Frank's objective is to coach people on how to build a life of "responsible wealth." Frank believes people are on two parallel paths financially: wealth protection and wealth building. His process assists people in navigating through these paths as efficiently and effectively as possible. In order to achieve a life of responsible wealth, both paths must be aligned.

While 2014 into 2015 posed challenges and continuous demonstrations of how my sinful human nature will always want to resist my Christian walk, Dave Suckey proved to be something I didn't think anyone other than Frank could be: both highly intelligent in matters of finance but also immensely honest. Though I call him a "young man," Dave's got a family of his own and is 40, so it's all relative. Roughly 20 years separate us in age, so I can't quite figure out if he is the son I never had or a long-lost brother. Maybe he's a little bit of both. Whichever the case, he's one of those God-placed people who has helped me to keep the spiritual ship righted. He aids in discerning which voices in my life come from the imperfect and broken me, and which are sent by My Maker.

> *"Three conditions are necessary for Penance:*
> *contrition, which is sorrow for sin,*
> *together with a purpose of amendment;*
> *confession of sins without any omission;*
> *and satisfaction by means of good works."*
> *- Saint Thomas Aquinas*

When we first published Confessions of a Wall Street Whiz Kid in 2011, I never envisioned a second edition, let alone a third. But four years later, the third edition is here. I would like to say it's the final edition, but I'll borrow from the old adage "never say never" and just note that I don't foresee a number four any time soon.

As previously noted, I ended Grandich Publications and virtually all involvement with the metals and mining industry at the end of 2013, continuing to write only for my long-time friend and one of Canada's most recognized financial journalists, Mr. Michael Campbell of MoneyTalks.net.

For the first time since it was founded 12 years earlier, in 2013 Trinity Financial Sports & Entertainment Management Company became my main livelihood. As 2014 unfolded, the good Lord would pour out many blessings, including not only greatly increased interest in my services by professional athletes, teams and agencies, but from the general public, too. Becoming a regular weekly commentator on Relevant Radio's number-one-most-listened-to program, The Drew Mariani Show, not only led to interest from around the country, but it also brought to light some unforeseen confusion that helped lead to an important business restructuring and the creation of my newest venture.

Though I had noted in all my marketing that Trinity Financial worked with the general public—not just professional athletes and entertainers, I found that many assumed because of the company name that I devoted my professional work exclusively to the rich and famous. As a result, in early 2015 I made the decision to form a new parent company, Peter Grandich & Company, and made Trinity Financial a division of PG&C so the members of the general public would be clear that they were every bit as important to me and my business as professional athletes. Around the same time, two factors became evident to me.

First, I came to know that writing and publishing Confessions of a Wall Street Whiz Kid was part of my penance for the way I had lived some of my business and personal life through 2013. For non-Catholic readers, the sacrament of penance is a self-imposed repentance where one confesses his or her sins and repents—really has a conversion of spirit—for the sins he or she has committed. It comes from the same root word as penitentiary; think of it as a way to help free ourselves from the prison of sin. Penance assists us in overcoming obstacles and temptations which are particularly troubling, and is one of the Seven Sacraments. Of all the sacraments, it is the most personal because it is between us and God. Ultimately, it is Jesus' sacrifice that frees us from sin—He paid the price for our sins. But by accepting His sacrifice and repenting there is forgiveness and absolution of sins, and ultimately it restores us to a place where we can experience God's grace, which I need today more than ever.

While some of the details of my sinful life have been published herein, the rest shall remain between me and God. In the end, however, I've been led to share the financial revelations that have been shown to me during my penance. These divulgences don't make me mightier than my peers, nor do they show me to be financially superior. In fact, it took multiple servings of humble pie before I could dish out these truths. What's important is that I believe God not only wants me to share these truths, but He expects me to share them as a way to help others become free of the trappings of the accumulation of wealth and everything the lifestyle brings.

The other fact that became painfully obvious to me was that as much as I personally enjoyed working with Michael Campbell, I needed to once-and-for-all end my ties to Canada and the mining industry. The Land of the Loonie would need to return to a place from whence comes refreshing chilled air masses to cool hot summer days; not a place where any of my day-to-day business life was focused. So with a heavy heart, I resigned as Senior Commentator for MoneyTalks and focused 100 percent of my efforts south of the border that separates two of the greatest countries in the world.

With a new parent company to act as the umbrella for all my business dealings (including a new Registered Investment Advisory company I just formed, Sageness Advisors), a final severing of business ties to Canada and the mining industry, and a life filled with Godly people, it seems that I'm on track to live my life to its fullest. As someone who once hid under the covers in fear of even getting out of bed, I know that being able to recognize God's voice is the key to that fullness and joy. Sadly, many of us hear His voice regularly but fail to listen. Not me—not any more. The people He has placed in my life—my wife Mary, Bill Wegner, George McGovern, Frank Congilose, and the rest—are tools given to me by a loving Father, for which I am grateful. I have never looked forward to each new day as I do now that I am in my last year before being officially old. Here's hoping 60 is the new 50.

Chapter 16

Still Making it the "Old-Fashioned" Way

"In the movie 'Wall Street' I play Gordon Gekko,
a greedy corporate executive who cheated to profit
while innocent investors lost their savings.
The movie was fiction, but the problem is real."
- Michael Douglas

By now, you've learned I was no perfect angel during my several decades of working in and around Wall Street. I remind myself and people I meet that were it not for the grace of God, I would still be turning the Ten Commandments into the Ten Suggestions. Unfortunately, the street where I first began my profession has gone from bad to worse.

Just before the great bull market began in the early 80s, a well-known brokerage firm employed legendary actor John Houseman as their pitch man, and he ended their commercials with the same line every time, "They make money the old-fashioned way... they eaaaaaarn it." We used to joke back in my stock brokerage days that they should change the last part to "...they churn it." (Churning, for those who may not know, is a term used on Wall Street that describes how brokers create transactions simply to create commissions.) Unfortunately for the general public, not only does this reckless, tasteless, insiders' "joke" remain unknown to everyday hardworking lay people, but far too many on Wall Street continue to make money as they have done for decades – illicitly. What doesn't help is our modern technology, which allows them to do so without breaking any current laws, a feat that would surely impress some of the best crooks who ever applied their trade through Wall and Broad.

Here's an example of how technology helps what I have to call "legal theft." Just last year, we learned that several financial groups spent hundreds of millions of dollars laying fiber optic cables so they could "legally" get in front of stock orders, buying what those orders were about to buy, and then re-selling the securities to those same buyers just a millisecond later at a penny or two per share profit. I think society's ignorance of these deals (or quite frankly, the assumption that beating others on Wall Street is no crime) is why there was no uprising to demand a change to this method. So, let me put this in layman's terms and tell me if you still think this practice is ok. What these folks did and continue to do is the same as if they knew you were going shopping, saw your shopping list, bought up everything on your list, and then restocked the shelves with your items at a penny or two higher than what they bought the items for... knowing you were walking in the store, pushing your cart and the carefully-prepared items were guaranteed to be bought.

Another example of the financial industry making money the old-fashioned way was the sub-prime mortgage fiasco which took place less than a decade ago. It was, in my opinion, the greatest financial crisis in our country's history and a major cause of the recession of 2007-09. Hundreds of billions of dollars, if not a trillion or more, were lost because financial institutions around the world (led by U.S. firms) sold mortgage-related products that they knew would fail. Furthermore, the financial institutions actually took the other side of the sale.

I truly believe the general public's lack of understanding of these transactions (or should say, transgressions) is the reason that not one high-ranking official of any financial institution was found guilty of these criminal acts. What occurred in the sub-prime mortgage crisis would be like if GM, Ford and Chrysler had sold cars that they *knew* would crash and then bought life insurance on the new owners so when they crashed and died, the car companies could profit twice. Trust me, if this was on the news tonight, the public would be up in arms and the car company executives would be going to jail. Yet, that is what happened, and almost none of the financial execs involved are being held legally accountable.

What would you think of a game where the rules were vague, changed every day without your knowledge, and there was no way to discern how to win? How would it make you feel to find out that not only do most other players have hidden agendas and allegiances, but they also have secret sources of information and much faster playing pieces than you? Given these circumstances, most people would choose not to play. It's too bad, then, that most are already playing this stacked deck one way or another with their finances.

I tell people that when I first became a stockbroker in 1984, the playing board was already tilted against the general public. Now it's even worse. I believe 99 percent of the public has a better chance of hitting the lottery than beating the market trading stocks on their own. Trust me, no matter what some crazy guy with a questionable past (who makes all sorts of noises on his daily TV show and yells "BOO-YAH!") likes to tell you, the game is rigged and only one in 100 people might make a buck. The rest usually lose, and some lose bigger than others.

Talking like this about the financial services industry has not exactly won me Mr. Congeniality. It's put an end to the Christmas party invitations from financial firms, brought me ridicule from many so-called "financial advisers," and my honest revelation is often far too "honest" a viewpoint for the general public to accept. Despite this, I continue to point out that:

- Traditional financial planning is doomed to fail;
- The vast majority of money managers fall short in performance;
- "Market timing" is nothing more than a cuckoo clock;
- Most in wealth management end up moving your wealth one way and theirs another;
- Cash flow—not net worth—is king.

If you were in need of surgery to save your life, would you allow a doctor to operate on you who failed 80 percent of the time compared to his or her peers? If you found yourself in legal trouble, would you want an attorney who failed to achieve what 80 percent of other attorneys managed to obtain for their clients? If you said yes, stop reading now. If you said no, I'll share another tidbit: 80 percent of professional money managers failed to match the performance of simply putting money in a basic, low cost index fund. Odds are good that your investment funds are being managed by the 80 percent—**not** the 20 percent. Before you run to find one of the 20-percenters, know that in all likelihood their "winning streak" will soon end like mine did, and they will join the 80-percenters going forward.

Dislike me yet?

Do you know how people of wealth obtained it? Most got it one of these three ways:

- Inheritance,
- Business ownership, or
- Buying and selling commercial real estate.

Despite the stock market being the investment of choice for the majority of people, I have discovered that its role in creating wealth tends to be limited to:

- Investors who get to be insiders at the earliest part of the food chain;
- Members of senior management who are granted stock options at much lower prices than you can purchase shares for;
- Financial sales people who sell financial products.

Still with me? If I haven't lost you yet, this next part could do the trick.

Wall Street has spent tens of billions of dollars creating an image of success when in fact, the vast majority of investors fall way short of their hopes and dreams. As I detailed in Chapter 12, traditional financial planning—a practice that today may come with lots of computer-generated graphics, statistics and bells and whistles—is destined to fail or fall far short of the intended goals. It's not because of dishonesty or a lack of skills; I'm certain that the vast majority of financial advisors in the U.S. get up each morning and hope to do an honest day's worth of work. Unfortunately, the very disclaimers given to their clients have the candid answers to their possibilities, albeit in legal mumbo jumbo that most don't comprehend or choose to ignore. It's the part that includes the phrase "past performance is no assurance of future results..." What it amounts to is something it took me 30 years to conclude: no one among us knows the future and almost all will not reach the theoretical returns built into the plan.

The straws that break the camel's back as to why so many investors don't come close to achieving their financial goals are these three commonalities found within the financial services industry:

1. The bulk of a financial advisor's education is geared toward getting his or her license. After that, much of the time is spent on product and sales training;

2. Hubris and arrogance of the client and/or the advisor (I'm guilty!) lead to decisions based on emotions versus academics and/or a proven process;

3. People buy because of greed and sell due to fear.

Show me an investor who has not obtained the financial success that he or she thought was once likely and I'll show you that he or she:

- Was way too dependent on just equities to increase wealth;
- Had a financial plan that depended on factors no one can consistently and correctly forecast over time;
- Had an advisor who was far better trained in sales than how money really works.

Over the bulk of my career, I travelled around the world speaking at investment conferences. It didn't take long before I concluded one critical factor about the lion's share of all the attendees: most came not to learn something new or different, but rather just to get confirmation of what they already believed. This phenomenon plays right into the hands of many who work in the financial world because when it comes to advisors, there are only two types:

1. Those who say what they think, and
2. Those who say what they think you want to hear... and it sells.

I'm here to say what I think. In an industry where you're truly only as good as your last call, falling on my face the last few times was truly sobering. With ego and pocketbook deflated, I finally practice what my financial mentor has preached to me for nearly 15 years. If you come away with just one realization after reading this book, I hope it is this: *Cash flow is for YOU; net worth is what you leave for SOMEONE ELSE.*

Got that? *Cash flow* (as described in chapter 12) is what you use now and will continue to use in retirement to pay your bills, go out to dinner, pay for health care and generally support your lifestyle. Cash flow is your paycheck. *Net worth*, on the other hand, is a number that reflects your overall wealth. Add up the value of all your investments and all your stuff, and that number equals your net worth. But the holdings that make up that number are often tied up in assets or investments such as stocks, bonds, real estate, or gold, and they are not liquid. You can't use shares of stocks to pay the mortgage. First, you have to liquidate those shares at which time your financial services professional gets a fee, then you pay a hefty tax on the capital gain between what the share is worth now and what it was worth when you first acquired it, and finally you can use the proceeds of that transaction to pay your bills. So, after your advisor and Uncle Sam get their cut, you can create a lifestyle with the rest...assuming that it's worth more today than when you bought it, and events of the past have proven that increase is certainly not anything that can be guaranteed.

Show me a business that failed and I'll almost certainly show you a business that lacked proper cash flow. That is not dissimilar to you running the business of your life in retirement—poor cash flow will make your retirement plan a failure. Yet, the financial world has brain-washed investors into thinking net worth is the key to financial success. How many times have you seen that commercial of a person carrying their "retirement number"? You know... that mythical net-worth figure that's supposed to assure a comfortable post-career lifestyle? It's not the failure to reach the number that often causes the plan to flop as much as it is a misguided obsession with net worth as the scorecard of wealth.

Though net worth may be a valuable yardstick for some things, in retirement what really matters are cash flow and after-tax income. Yet, almost all typical financial plans use reverse engineering that is only intended to preserve principal net worth while living off of interest. The reverse engineering begins with how much income a person thinks he or she will need, and then backs out "the number." If a person wants to retire on $125,000 a year (which is a total guess, by the way), this approach assumes one needs a net worth of roughly $2.5 million to avoid dipping into principal. That's based on the formula adopted industry-wide which assumes a retirement portfolio will yield about four to five percent per year in income without diminishing principal.

Think about that for a moment. They're *counting* on four to five percent gain year after year after year. Raise your hand if, like me, you've taken such heavy losses some years that you'd be happy that some of your investments were worth only five percent less than when you bought them? Letting your lifestyle in retirement rest on the assumption that your portfolio will yield four or five percent per year is foolhardy, in my opinion.

The investment industry promotes this magic number notion because it's in the business of accumulating assets to manage. Financial institutions are merely intermediaries; they just connect people and businesses with money and get paid very well as middlemen. The more they connect investors with investments, the more money they make. There is a disincentive to showing clients how they may be able to spend some of their principal and still achieve their goals.

They use the fear of outliving one's assets to continue this pattern that benefits them over their clients. In addition to using fear as a motivation, the financial services industry counts on the fact that the average investor is a creature of habit. Despite the likelihood that you may now conclude the financial services industry isn't all it's cracked up to be, their constant barrage of marketing combined with your human nature to default to what makes you comfortable (along with a dose of procrastination), are strong forces that many can't overcome. Like any other bad habit, many people just do what they've always done.

Instead of staying on that hamster wheel, I suggest focusing on a process to build and protect wealth with efficiency at the core, which can lead to a better quality of life. Use an academic approach to asset management and protection, not an emotional one based upon what some product may or may not have done in the past.

It may have taken three decades but with the help of my financial mentor, Frank Congilose, I finally came to the realization that any good financial advisor must demonstrate to his or her clients how critical their lives require financial balance to achieve personal fulfillment. *True wealth management demands improving a client's quality of life, and cash flow will determine that quality—not net worth.* Many people boast substantial net worth but have poor cash flow and thus feel poor. What is the benefit of having $2.5 million worth of anything if you still can't pay your bills?

Since the industry and much of its sales force focus mainly on the sale of products, this kind of education fails miserably in teaching its clientele how to reduce and eliminate many of the wealth-eroding factors faced in today's world. If financial advisors focused on a process that demonstrates efficiency, cost recovery, asset protection, asset utilization and then wealth building, the advisors and their clients would be much better off. I believe that real wealth is not achieved by exotic financial products or complicated strategies, but instead it is derived from making the most of the opportunities that are often overlooked and underutilized.

If you made it this far, let me congratulate you. I suspect only a small minority of people who began reading this book have read through up until now. That's okay. I've come to accept the fact that only a few will really appreciate hearing the brutal truth, while the rest will still be prime targets of an industry that has spent tens of billions of dollars marketing an ungodly and unethical belief of the lie that more money equals more happiness.

Yes sir, it's still the old-fashioned way.

Chapter 17

The Seven Deadly Sins of Finance

I said before that part of my penance was to take my past sins in matters of finance and turn them into serving the greater good. And just so we're absolutely clear, I'm not speaking from some greater-than-thou mountain top: I, too, have lost millions more than once...and *they* call *me* the Wall Street Whiz Kid. But, after millions in personal losses and more red ink in the columns of former clients and readers who I'm certain wish they had never heard of me, I have come to learn a thing or two. Ironically, it is my 30-plus years of being an expert on what *not to do* that allows me now to be able to suggest what *to do*. Through my financial sinning, confession, contrition and penance, I have discovered that there are seven deadly sins on matters of finance that if eliminated, would render most of us a heck of a lot better off.

In theology, the "seven deadly sins" is a classification system that has been used for thousands of years to teach Christians about humanity's tendency to sin. They are first found in the

Old Testament book of Proverbs. Though the wording has been modernized over the centuries, the concepts remain the same. The sins are usually described as wrath, greed, sloth, pride, lust, envy and gluttony. If we're honest with ourselves, we can all relate to one (or all) of them.

In the financial world, I believe there are seven deadly sins of matters of finance...categories of vices into which most all of our financial wrongdoings fall. They are:
1. Believing you can predict future market movements
2. Utilizing traditional financial planning methods which are doomed to fail
3. Assuming financial "advice" is unbiased and objective
4. Exhibiting arrogance
5. Believing more money equals more happiness
6. Participating in mental anguish
7. Procrastination

After committing all seven of these sins more than once over the past 30 years, my financial mentor, Frank Congilose, was finally able to make me realize the error of my ways and repent. Now, my penance is to humble myself by publicly sharing this. While not easy at first, for me it's become a burning desire like that of a recovering addict who doesn't want to see others make the same bad mistakes. I believe recognizing these seven pitfalls is a necessary step we all must take before we can truly reach our financial goals. So let's go through them one by one.

Number 1: Believing you can predict future market movements

Being called the Wall Street Whiz Kid for forecasting many significant market moves did a lot for my ego, but in the end, it really hurt my personal wealth. Neither I nor anyone else can correctly forecast future moves consistently and what's more, we eventually realize we put our pants on one leg at a time just like everybody else. Whoever the financial media may be featuring today as a soothsayer will likely end up in the "what was his name?" bin down the road. Though some folks can forecast accurately every now and again, nobody can predict future market movements on a regular basis and thinking you (or your financial advisor) can will ultimately lead to financial damnation.

As noted earlier, 80 percent of money managers can't even equal the performance of a simple equity index fund. In bonds, it's 85 percent. This is not to say that for some people, having managed money as part of an overall strategy is wrong. But to assume that the majority of financial advisors will deliver on performance is truly a monetary crime.

Number 2: Utilizing traditional financial planning methods which are doomed to fail

I've been blessed to be involved with professional athletes and teams for about 15 years. While I've learned many things during this period, none was more important than the fact that all teams have written plans. Many call it a play book. It's a pre-planned, well-thought-out strategy for winning the game. Yet today, the majority of people don't have a written financial plan for "winning the game." And the ones who do have no real idea that the game was lost even before the coin toss.

When I first started in the business, a legal pad and a pen were all I needed when meeting with a potential client. Today, massive amounts of slick advertising material and a computer-generated analysis of one's finances with all sorts of charts and graphs are the norm. But much—if not all—

is just propaganda because most of what's called financial planning is doomed to fail. (Go back to chapter 12 if you need a refresher on why.)

Whether it's *needs-based planning* which focuses on meeting an individual goal like paying for college or retirement, or the formulation of an all-encompassing life and death proposition, all these so-called plans are dead on arrival, in my opinion. Want proof? Simply go to the end of the plan and see for yourself, if you take the time and can comprehend the legal disclaimer that is surely incorporated somewhere in the written analysis ...it will be very small print and almost certainly will not have been reviewed in any detail. It goes something like this, "Past performance is no assurance of future results..." Yet in most plans, an investment product's past performance is projected out over a number of years suggesting similar returns in the future. If only life was that simple.

But using an "anticipated rate of return" is not only standard in most financial planning, it's limited to that. I was guilty of primarily focusing on that, too, so don't beat yourself up for being among the fiscal sinners. What I have found, however, is that by adding "rate of accumulation" and "rate of distribution" to your plan, it now has a far better opportunity to succeed. Hopefully you will discover as I did that *rate of accumulation* is far more important than the heavily touted and "guesstimated" *rate of return*. Increasing the rate you accumulate money (i.e., rate of saving) through cash flow efficiencies and financial strategies that identify where you are losing money (and doing all this without having to change your lifestyle), is one of the two keys to the only process I have ever learned that really works.

The other key is "rate of distribution." By using efficient distribution strategies, you can increase retirement income by 20 to 40 percent with the same asset base. This allows one to secure a quality of life by removing the fear of outliving your money.

In addition to the three R's (rate of accumulation, rate of distribution, and rate of return), it's critical that a financial plan have parallel paths that equally secure wealth building as well as wealth protection. Unfriendly creditors and a host of real life events can greatly impact even the best of wealth building plans. Though often overlooked in most traditional financial plans, it is of paramount importance to maintain cash flow and control by employing a number of legal processes, terms and conditions.

Number 3: Assuming financial "advice" is unbiased and objective

Among the deadliest of the seven sins is the belief that the financial institutions (and the media that makes a living off them) are on your side.

Let's first be clear: yours truly didn't always act 100 percent in the best interests of clients. Being a legend in my own mind, turning the Ten Commandments into the Ten Suggestions while being the Chairman and CEO of the Me, Myself and I Society certainly gives me first-hand experience in this financial transgression.

Earlier, I told the story of when, in August of 1987, I forecasted a stock market crash and my boss at the brokerage firm wanted me to retract it or resign. I spoke about his description of how most of the firm's clients would either not follow and/or not profit from my advice, and how none of that would lead to sales and profits for the firm. From a sales point of view, he was correct.

If you believe financial institutions exist for your benefit and not theirs, let me ask you this: if the Archangel Gabriel appeared to every person in charge of every financial institution's investment strategy and said God Himself had sent Gabriel to warn of a terrible market crash to come, even if the strategist believed Gabriel was right, do you honestly think his superiors would allow him to issue a major sell off of most, if not all equities?

If you answered yes, I'm surprised you made it this far. If you answered no, then ask yourself how you will overcome the biases and conflicts of interest that you're up against. Google stories on the misdeeds of financial institutions and you'll have countless hours of reading material of real-life stories that continue basically unabated today. Again I remind you: the deck is stacked against you.

Number 4: There is one deadly sin that both investor and advisor commit: Arrogance.

Suffice it to say that I took Number 4 to new heights. When a market didn't do what I predicted, the market got it wrong, not me! Often times, good decision making drowned in a sea of stinking, selfish arrogance. Furthermore, ego allowed emotions to overpower strategic pre-planning. Both investors and advisors commit this narcissistic crime of letting their pride and ego get in the way, preventing them from admitting that they made a wrong call. And even more mortal of a sin, their hubris prevents them from taking corrective measures because that would really accentuate their misgivings.

The Bible says, "Haughtiness goes before destruction" – Proverbs 18:12, and just in case you were wondering, the dictionary lists arrogance, hubris, pride and conceit as synonyms for haughtiness. If you want to achieve financial success, I implore you to check your financial chutzpah at the door. Egos get in the way of good financial results.

Number 5: The big lie: more money equals more happiness

Financial institutions' advertisements all have one theme – engage their services and your dreams will come true. While they never actually say they will reach your goals, all their slick ads elude to that result. I can tell you the percentage of goals reached is far higher for the financial institutions than it is for their clientele.

When you strip away all the crafty wording, the essence of the financial institutions' marketing is that they can increase your net worth through a variety of products and services. This, in turn, will allow you to have the monies for whatever your goals may be.

A couple hundred years ago, the French philosopher Voltaire wrote, "Don't think money does everything or you are going to end up doing everything for money." How right he was. I know firsthand how god can be spelled: M-O-N-E-Y. For the first half of my career, I worshipped it. But it never brought lasting happiness. It took the loss of millions of dollars (more than once), two debilitating bouts of depression, numerous angels and the incredible love of family and friends for me to finally realize that money was not my God, and it is far less important than I and the world give it credit for. I truly hope such hard lessons aren't required for you to conclude the same.

Number 6: Participating in mental anguish

I started this journey with the making of a tidy sum only to lose it to a penny stockbroker. Then as a stockbroker myself, I not only lost clients' money over and over again, but mine, too. While the financial ramifications from the losses were nothing to sneeze at, the mental anguish was much worse. Sure, I made money, too, but I never beat myself up over that.

While I believe financial advisors don't wake up each morning hoping to lose their clients' monies, the end result of the business is that losses are common. And because of the way that most advisors are groomed for the business, they never have to live with the mental anguish of losing money. It's just all in a day's work. But for me and for many people whose financial futures are on the line, the mental pain persists long after the financial woes subside.

As I have said before, one of the best ways to avoid this sin against your financial future is to never invest (i.e., "gamble") more than you can afford to lose. It greatly decreases any potential to ruminate on your losses.

Number 7: Procrastination

Napoleon Hill, legendary personal success guru and author of Think and Grow Rich, one of the best-selling books of all time, defined procrastination as, "the bad habit of putting off until the day after tomorrow what should have been done the day before yesterday." Though he wasn't talking specifically about finances, the concept fits.

Psychologists say procrastination reflects man's personal struggle with self-control. If that's true, we all need to take more control over our finances. Time is indeed money, and though most investors and professionals know little about them, Lost Opportunity Costs (LOCs) and Velocity of Money (VOM), as explained in chapter 12, are critical factors in obtaining wealth. Putting off employing these "secret weapons" is not just foolhardy, but I think fiscally sinful. I know, I know, it's easy to get distracted. And nobody likes to dive into the things of finance they either dislike or know little about. That's when procrastination becomes sinful for most investors.

People delay making decisions for a number of reasons. Sometimes, extra steps in the process rightfully slow the decision. Sometimes, life just gets in the way. Whether it's a comfort level that never materializes, the fear of making the wrong move, divine intervention or many other excuses, most people believe they can put off until tomorrow (or next week, next month, next year) making decisions relating to their financial futures. What they don't take into consideration is the penalty they will pay for this financial wrongdoing.

"And you will know the truth, and the truth will set you free."
- John 8:32

Chapter 18

Three Strikes. I'm Out of Sports.

"Integrity is choosing your thoughts and actions based on
values rather than personal gain."
' *- Chris Karcher*

As you know, I co-founded TFSEM back in 2001 with Lee Rouson, the former NY Giants two-time Super Bowl champion running back. For almost two decades, I was blessed to work with numerous active and retired professional athletes, including 13 years with NY Giants players and coaches. I lived most guys' sports fantasies on a regular basis. Trust me, I could start telling you stories about them on a Monday, and by Sunday I wouldn't come close to being finished.

The 2015 season was my last one with the Giants. By then, I started to see not only my age but also the color of my skin as a challenge both personally and in business. I was as old as many of the players' grandfathers, and as a white guy from the Bronx, I found it more and more difficult to earn the trust of these young Black men. American media and our out-of-control, politically-correct society will never say it but I will: reverse prejudice is real.

Strike One.

Though my work ended with professional teams, I still maintained a very active business and personal life with individual athletes. I hosted several meet-and-greets at my Spring Lake, NJ office, and I sponsored a number of athletes at civic, business and recreational events.

When the NFL's Colin Kaepernick and athletes in other sports started taking a knee and displaying what I believe to be blatant disrespect for the United States during the National Anthem, I and millions of other Americans took offense. The difference in my case, however, was that my business life was almost immediately negatively impacted. The fact that I openly spoke out against it only added to the furor I experienced from some in the sports world.

Strike Two.

While the COVID-19 pandemic brought a halt to any and all sports-related marketing and business development, the entrance of the Black Lives Matter (BLM) movement into the forefront of daily life and the attacks on any and all who dared to speak out against it, led me to make one of the toughest decisions of my life.

As a devout Catholic Christian, how could I engage with professional athletes and teams who openly and loudly supported an organization that preached acceptance of politically-correct issues that directly contradict my faith?

I'm not talking about justice or equality; these are Biblical concepts. God created us alike and in His image, and He loves us all equally. The Bible says:

There is no difference between Jew and Gentile—the same Lord is Lord of all and richly blesses all who call on him. - Romans 10:12

God shows no partiality, but in every nation anyone who fears him and does what is right is acceptable to him. - Acts 10:34-35

There is neither Jew nor Greek, there is neither slave nor free, there is no male and female, for you are all one in Christ Jesus. - Galatians 3:28

Based on everything I have learned in life and in church, I know that society does not determine our value. God does.

My beef with BLM isn't about social justice, it's some of the lesser-known beliefs the organization espoused which directly conflict with my Christianity. Because the BLM movement so openly promotes lifestyles and concepts which are contradictory to the teachings of the Bible and the tenets of my faith, I felt it would be the ultimate in hypocrisy to wear my faith on one sleeve and a BLM armband on the other.

I aggressively wrote and spoke about this and before too long, clients and other interested parties departed, expressing dismay over my stance.

One professional athlete with whom I had developed a personal relationship came to discuss the BLM topic with me and we went to lunch. (To his credit, I respect and appreciate the fact that he didn't just drop me like a hot potato. He reached out to discuss his views and hear mine—a strategy that few people employ today.)

During our meal, he tried to compassionately school me on his side of the argument and told me all of the reasons why I was wrong in my evaluation of the movement. I listened to everything he had to say and then asked him how he would feel if the waiter, cook and busboy came to our table and instead of serving us lunch, gave us a sermon of sorts about a social issue—any social issue? After 10 or 15 minutes, what would be his reaction?

He said, "Since I came here to eat, not to listen to them, I'd want my meal. What they do on their own time is up to them."

I agreed, saying that the restaurant is in the business of feeding people.

Similarly, I explained, he and the pro sports teams were in the entertainment business. Just like he wanted only to be served and fed by the restaurant, fans in stadiums and watching on TV—people who pay a lot of money to see him and others play a game they had loved since childhood—simply wanted to be entertained.

Studies show a number of reasons fans watch sports. Columbia Journalism Review reported that there are eight common motivations for sports fandom, among them: getting one's self-esteem from sports; watching because it's exciting; needing an escape from real-world troubles; and because sports provide a sense of belonging and a connection to a wider world.

So whether the fans are watching to relive their glory days playing high school ball or because they are hoping to get away from the world for a few hours, nobody's tuning in to be lectured about a social issue—any social issue.

I noted that what he did on his time was his business, but his job was to play and people watch because they want to see him play (and hopefully win) at the game. I added that these were people who sunk a pretty penny into his career by paying for tickets, buying a jersey with his number on it, and otherwise financially supporting his livelihood; and he'd been paid handsomely to do it.

I told him that I believed what he was doing during the game was akin to the waiter and busboy campaigning instead of serving our meal. I added that if players protested before or after the game, most viewers wouldn't have a problem with it. But being forced to participate in their social statement didn't fall into the category of entertainment.

He thought about it for a moment and agreed. But the following week he was back on the field making a social statement. It was that response that clinched my decision to end that part of my life.

Strike Three.

In the months that followed, I gave away to worthy causes and good people tens of thousands of dollars of sports memorabilia, and I closed the books on Trinity Financial Sports and Entertainment Management Company.

Chapter 19

The Absolutely Final Chapter. No, Really; This Is It.

Really.

It's truly hard to believe that it's been a decade since the first edition of this book was issued. Never did I imagine multiple editions, let alone a fifth and "final" edition. (I know, I know; you've heard that before. But for all of the reasons I've already detailed, this is really it.).

Before I go, I wouldn't be the "Wall Street Whiz Kid" if I didn't prognosticate one last time about what I anticipate of us for the foreseeable future. Keep in mind, though, that no one (including yours truly) knows the future except Almighty God. Anyone who claims to be able to peer into their crystal ball and predict the financial future will only become an expert on how to eat lots of broken glass.

I wasn't around just before America's civil war (though some days I feel old enough to have been), but I can't believe the country could have been much more divided than it is right now. The middle class has been pounded to near extinction; and so has the middle ground on nearly every social and political opinion. Increasingly, it seems that there is only the extreme left and the far right, with little appetite for any views that that may lie between the two. Up until now, Wall Street had been able to stay insulated from the chaos and division that Main Street USA is experiencing, but if the division and disharmony continues, that separation of Wall Street from Main Street won't last and the stock market will fall back to earth... hard.

Sadly, America has made a sharp turn to the left and I believe some form of socialism is already being seeded. This is not a mere few degrees to the left—it's a well-funded and strongly backed 90-degree left attack that is supported by those who want no part of the Judeo-Christian beliefs that made this a country great.

Now let me lose several more readers by stating the following: In 2020, we witnessed a four-year conspiracy to overthrow a duly-elected president come to a head, and we obtained a new president by putting up a candidate through a scheme the likes of which the writers of "Weekend At Bernie's" and "The Sting" would be envious.

I believe the demonic darkness engulfing our nation has been led by billionaire globalist evildoers. These globalist elites, along with the Deep State and social media tyrants of Silicon Valley, are rich, influential, arrogant and the greatest hypocrites ever to roam the earth. They no longer hide in the shadows but instead publicly flaunt their capture of our government, electoral systems, financial systems, mainstream media, social media, and health care system.

They have reviewed the intellectual, ethical, and mathematical aptitude of the masses and found them greatly lacking. So, they had no fear of significant pushback as they actively took part in a questionable presidential election, trashing the Constitution, destroying small business owners, impoverishing what remains of the middle class, and imposing totalitarian restrictions upon a compliant and obedient population.

A nation once populated by independent minded, self-reliant, frontiersmen has rotted from within, as the country is now populated by millions of weak-minded, submissive, docile sheep who allow themselves to be bullied and propagandized into paralysis while texting, tweeting and posting their every mindless thought to "followers." It's nothing less than sad.

Having been in and around the financial markets for nearly 40 years, I can sense we're in the biggest bubble in history. About 10 percent of society is doing financially well with the higher layers within that percentage doing fantastically, while the remaining 90 percent among us struggle to stay afloat or have already succumbed to the floodwaters. The excess speculation already witnessed in general equities has now spilled over to things like Bitcoin, where professional money managers now claim its real value is nearly 20 times greater than the current price. (They used to throw penny stock brokers out of the business if they sold stocks promising the same upside potential).

The greatest challenge of bubbles, however, is that they can really only be identified after the fact. A bubble-like market can remain aloft far longer and higher than its naysayers. As long as the market's climax is still not well known, there is always a ready source of market defenders who adamantly share "why this time it's different." It takes the passage of time and a clear peak in price to convince the vast majority of market participants that a bubble did indeed take place. Sadly, by then, many have seen their dreams turn into living nightmares and any financial wealth flushed down the tubes with the markets.

Finally, I end by reminding you that America has been robbing Peter to pay Paul, and Peter has all but gone broke doing so. One day (and don't ask me when) when our 24/7 printing presses will no longer be able to keep printing money without paying a dear price, an enormous debt bill will finally come due and the harsh, austere life that follows will be no picnic. Simply put, the debt we're racking up as a nation is a tab someone we love and care about is going to be stuck with (one of the only upsides to getting old is that my generation will not have to pay this toll).

I reiterate what's been said in previous chapters: whether you're talking about the finances of the federal government or the finances of your household budget, always remember that debt is bad. There is not one positive verse in the Bible on debt. God knew what it would lead to, and unfortunately, America will find out sooner than you think.

The Bottom Line:

I continue to advocate for ratcheting back spending to live a financially responsible lifestyle, and I remind all who will listen to this Wall Street Geezer that living within one's means (or even better, being debt free), is the only way to true financial freedom, no matter what your income or savings level.

Thank you for reading my book. I pray my testimony here might help you or someone you love to challenge the way you think about life, adversity and finances, and that it gives glory to the Creator of all that is good in the Universe.

> *"Do not conform to the pattern of this world,*
> *but let God transform you into a new person*
> *by changing the way you think."*
>
> *- Romans 12:2*

Appendix

Athletes in Action
George McGovern, Area Director
29 Beechwood Rd.
Oradell, NJ 07649
201-385-9416
www.athletesinactionnyc.org

Fellowship of Christian Athletes of New Jersey (FCA)
Harry Flaherty, State Director
6 Drummond Place, Suite 2
Red Bank, NJ 07701
732-219-5797
hflaherty@fca.org
www.fcanj.org

Good News International Ministries
Bill Wegner, Founder
P.O. Box 302
Howell, NJ 07731
1-800-430-0586
goodnewsinternational@cybercomm.net
www.GoodNewsInternational.net

The Institute of Responsible Wealth
> *Frank J. Congilose*
> 2431 Atlantic Avenue
> Manasquan, NJ 08736
> 732-528-4800
> www.IofRW.com

Muslim Investing Website
> The following link will provide a glimpse of the
> Islamic financial perspective that is currently
> employed in the Islamic countries
> http://muslim-investor.com/principles

No Labels Movement
> *Founded by former U.S. Comptroller David Walker*
> P.O. Box 25429
> Washington, DC 20027
> 202-588-1990
> www.nolabels.org

***The Third Jihad* documentary**
> Twelve-minute trailer
> http://www.thethirdjihad.com/12min.php

David Walker Video Links
> David Walker on CBS NEWS *60 Minutes* with Steve
> Kroft, aired May 1, 2007
> https://www.youtube.com/watch?v=U19_OkPRggE

> *I.O.U.S.A. The Movie* – The Thirty-Minute Version
> http://www.youtube.com/watch?v=O_TjBNjc9Bo

"Disco Pete" - Circa 1977. Taken in my parents apartment in Bronx, New York.

Me and one of my two all time-sports heroes, Joe Klecko. We're standing in front of the image of his No. 73 jersey, one of only three numbers to be retired by the Jets. (The other two were Joe Namath and Don Maynard.) Joe's jersey was retired in a halftime ceremony on December 26, 2005, and I was privileged to be on the field with him that day, too.

That's me getting a hug from the late Danny Aiello, my former Little League baseball coach and Oscar-nominated actor. Danny was one heck of a great singer, too.

That's my other all-time sports here on my right, former NY Ranger Nick Fotiu. To my left is former Ranger Ron Greschner and heavyweight "Gentleman" Gerry Cooney, one of the funniest guys I have ever met.

If every professional athlete was as caring and giving as this guy, former NY Giant Justin Tuck...Tuck spent a lot of time with a terminally-ill young fan, and this shot was taken in the boy's living room. To Justin's left is team chaplain George McGovern.

*On the Giants sidelines with Jeff Feagles, called
the most durable punter in NFL history.*

*Here I am with former NY Giant David Tyree, who is best
known for his incredible backwards "helmet catch" on the
Giants' final drive of Super Bowl XLII in 2008.*

I'm standing in front of the Big Blue Warrior Creed inside the Giants locker room.

On the sidelines with Giants placekicker Jay Feely.

Yes, friends, that is what the inside of the Giants locker room looks like. I am seen here clutching my Bible after a Giants Bible study in which I particiapted.

Me and my daughter, Tara. Yes, Daddy's little girl! She was probably 9 years old in this photo.

Below, that's her with Eli Manning of the Giants. She was 17 in that shot.

Hall-of-Famer "Broadway" Joe Namath, me, and the man who should be the next player inducted into the Hall of Fame, Joe Klecko.

Trinity Financial, Sports & Entertainment Management Company was born in 2001 with the help of my co-founder Lee Rouson, who is a former NY Giants running back and two-time Super Bowl Champion.

What a job I have! Here I am surrounded by the members of the Jets "New York Sack Exchange," the most feared defensive line in football. From left is Joe Klecko, Marty Lyons, Abdul Saalam and Mark Gastineau. Circa 2009.

On the pre-game sidelines with Marty Lyons (left) and Joe Klecko.

Super Bowl XLVII Champion and MVP Joe Flacco, then quarterback of the Baltimore Ravens.

Me with a group of men who literally changed (and helped save) my life. From left, Trinity co-founder and two-time Super Bowl champ Lee Rouson, Joe Klecko, and former Giant Keith Elias.

201

Standing outside of my office in Spring Lake, New Jersey.

With NY Jets legend Joe Klecko at the opening of my office in Spring Lake.

That's me with pro tag-team wrestling champions Road Warriors Hawk (left) and Animal, "The Legion of Doom." How tragic it was when Mike (Hawk) died suddenly in 2003. Joe (Animal) went on to compete and win after Hawk's death, often dedicating the win to his depart mate saying, "Hawk, this one was for you, brother!"

Yes, that's my bride, the former Mary Troy, flanked by the late Danny Aiello and me on our 30th wedding anniversary.

Here I am with former NY Jet Erik Coleman.

Me in front of one of my very favorite athlete's locker, that of Justin Tuck.

To my right is former NY Rangers Fan Favorite Nick Fotiu and on my left is former NJ Devil Ken Daneyko.

That's former Philadelphia Flyer Brian Propp, me and former NJ Devil Jim Dowd.

Here I am surrounded by Board Members Nick Fotiu, Ricky Aiello, Ray Lucas and Ron Greschner.

Me and Tony "Goose" Siragusa, a Jersey guy who spent 12 seasons as Defensive Tackle for the Colts and Ravens.

Here I am with former NY Rangers fan favorite Nick Fotiu.

Me with three-time Stanley Cup champion and Mr. Devil himself, Ken Daneyko.

This is me with Philadelphia Flyers Hall of Famer Brian Propp.

Here I am alongside Jim Dowd, who was a member of the first NJ Devils team to win a Stanley Cup in 1995.

With three-time Super Bowl champion Dan Klecko, who won two Super Bowls with the New England Patriots and another one with the Indianapolis Colts.

This is from one of our Christmas celebrations at my Spring Lake office, where we were joined by TV/radio personality Bill Spadea, former U.S. Women's National Soccer Team captain Christie Pearce Rampone and the talented wife/husband combo of former Olympic skater Sinead Kerr and two-time Stanley Cup winner Grant Marshall.

This is me with former boxer turned actor John Duddy, actor Ricky Aiello and our wives.

Standing alongside former Philadelphia Eagles linebacker and current Philadelphia sports broadcaster Garry Cobb.

There was a line outside of our door and down the sidewalk when we hosted NY Giants Super Bowl hero David Tyree for Big Blue Day at our office in Spring Lake.

Having a conversation with NY Giants Super Bowl hero David Tyree and former NFL running back Donald Brown.

Widely noted as the greatest defender in international women's soccer history, Christie Pearce Rampone is a former captain of the U.S. Women's National Team who won three Olympic Gold Medals and two FIFA Women's World Cup championships.

Here with five-time NY Giants Pro Bowler and current Assistant GM for the team, Jessie Armstead.

This is me with former NY Jets Joe Klecko, Greg Buttle and Dave Szott.

Endorsements

Peter Grandich has combined faith, intellect, insight and many life experiences into *Confessions of a Wall Street Whiz Kid*. This book is both an easy and entertaining read and very thought provoking.
    —Hon. David M. Walker, Former U.S. Comptroller General

There is nobody on Wall Street who is kinder than Peter. Listen to him and enjoy his book. Even when he is wrong (and everyone is at some time or another) you can be sure that Peter will give you honest advice.
    —John Crudele, Columnist, *New York Post*

In the world of finance, where far too often people speak in platitudes, Peter Grandich delivers a concise, intelligent, and at time humorous look at the markets. Peter may ruffle a few feathers, but his expertise should not be ignored. I was a fan long before I was his friend, but I am happy to be both at this point in my life!
    — Guy Adami, CNBC-TV Contributor

While I've benefitted from Peter's financial advice, the real gift was seeing God transform his life for the better. Having a heavenly wife didn't hurt him either.
    —Joe Klecko, Former NY Jet

Peter's honest and bold account shows that it is necessary for the Christ follower to lay down the very things we esteem above God Himself and that with God all things are possible-even a rich man entering the Kingdom of God.
    —David Tyree, Former NY Giant and author,
    More Than Just The Catch

Talk about a real knockout, my friend Peter Grandich has twice battled depression and has come out on top. His book deserves heavyweight recognition for his courage and willingness to share how he battled what life has thrown at him. Even during the darkest days, his priority has always been to help others.
    —"Gentleman" Gerry Cooney, Former Heavyweight Boxer

Former

I feel like I should put out an alert: Attention all investors- read this book before you make your next move. Peter Grandich has managed to distill a lifetime of experience and hard lessons learned into this important book. It will make and save you money.
—Michael Campbell, Host of Canada's *MoneyTalks*,
    on the Corus Radio Network

Peter has never been afraid to share the ups and down of his life. His story has both inspired and motivated me.
—Justin Tuck, NFL All-Pro

In *Confessions of a Wall Street Whiz Kid*, Peter Grandich reveals his personal journey, not just from rags to riches but from material wealth to spiritual wealth. His insights into the flawed nature of financial planning and the false god of retirement are alone worth the cover price. The ultimate treasure, he eloquently reminds us, lies not on earth, vulnerable to rust and thieves, but in the world that awaits us all.
— Jonathan Chevreau, *National Post* columnist and
    author, *Findependence Day*

In a world where fancy suits and Ivy League degrees are common, Peter Grandich took a most uncommon approach to finances and faith. He succeeded in both but not without battles along the boards and a couple of near game misconducts.
—Ken Daneyko, Three-time Stanley Cup Champion NJ Devil

Knowing Peter from childhood, I'm only too glad to suggest reading his book.
—Danny Aiello, Academy Award nominated actor and singer

Confessions of a Wall Street Whiz Kid is an absolute must for your spiritual library! Peter Grandich and his remarkable journey offer a powerful warning to those who put their trust in material things as well as great hope and inspiration for those trying to balance life's true priorities. This book will challenge you personally, make you think, and hopefully, set you on the path to true freedom and fulfillment.
—Drew Mariani, Nationally-Syndicated Radio Host and
    award winning director

It has been my pleasure to have known Peter Grandich now for thirty years and treasure him as a friend. Over the years I have come to enjoy his intelligence and wit, and appreciate his advice on financial matters. Most of all I am truly inspired by his ardent faith, his extraordinary generosity, and his compassion for those who have met misfortune in their lives. I welcome this book that will illustrate these and so many more attributes of Peter's makeup. However, let me make it clear that self praise is not the motive for his writing. Rather, he is driven to share in yet another way the many blessings that have come his way—even through the down times—and offer hope to those who may have been smitten by the hardships of life. It is my fervent hope and prayer that this book will indeed achieve these ends for the many.

—Very Rev. Brendan Williams, V.F.

I have never asked Peter for his financial expertise, and he may be a Wall Street Whiz Kid, but his greatest gift to me was his friendship.

—Ray Lucas, Former NFL Quarterback

Thirty years ago, I attended an investment club meeting chaired by Peter. I was impressed and hired him as a broker for my securities firm. He excelled beyond my wildest dreams to the point he is now the guru to athletes and business CEO's while enjoying a great walk with The Lord . I am honored to call him my friend. Well done, Peter.

— Bob Knapp

This book brings us back to being American again and remembering that our forefathers said "IN GOD WE TRUST." If Peter ran for president, he would have my vote.

—Ron Greschner, Former New York Ranger

Peter Grandich's story is truly a story of transformation, inspiration, and encouragement! Peter just doesn't talk the talk; he walks the walk each day being brought closer to God, surrendering his will to His...a 'Divine Ex-Change.'

—Lee Rouson, Two-time Super Bowl Champion NY Giant

What People Have Said

I first heard Peter on Relevant Radio and it was immediately clear his message was very different from conventional financial advisors and the mainstream media.

Peter spoke truth about finance, debt, consumerism and the investment industry to the detriment of his business so I was immediately intrigued. He has the rare commodity of real wisdom, financial and otherwise, rooted in both his faith and decades of experience. I have been personally blessed by Peter's faithfulness to the vocation God has called him to for the latter part of his career and that is to help people by speaking truth about finance and money matters in a biblical/Christian framework. It's not what people want to hear and it's also what we need to hear if we want to be on solid ground as individuals and as a nation.

Shortly after meeting Peter I had the pleasure of connecting with Dave Suckey and have been working with both of them as my most trusted financial advisors ever since. If you want to deal with real people who are authentic in their desire to help others in matters of finance, they are among the most talented and trustworthy people I have worked with in my 30+ year career. Good people, wise people and men who have built their business and more importantly their lives with integrity on a solid foundation of faith in God.

D.M. Henderson – NV

Peter Grandich is a one-of-kind gem in how he conducts his personal and professional life. I truly feel blessed to have known Peter for the past three years and wished that I had met him sooner. His passion to help others personally, spiritually, and financially manifests itself daily in his words and actions. His many years of wisdom, research, and integrity is rooted in his financial observations that has not only significantly improved my financial well-being, but has also proven to be so unique and refreshing to his industry that I would not recommend anyone else other than Peter Grandich and his company. Thank you, Peter.

R.F. – Monmouth Beach, NJ

Peter Grandich is an amazing individual with so many incredible talents. I believe he underestimates himself when you first meet him. His financial mind is amazing and his calm, cool, compassionate approach to life and business is both intriguing and uplifting. His knowledge of the thought process of people and his most sincere application of his faith to everyday life is extraordinary to say the least. He is the one person leaving you wanting to know more! I also admire the relationship he has with his wife and family.

A.M. – Eatontown, NJ

I have known Mr. Grandich for over 30 years. He has been a financial adviser, business partner and friend during that time. No one is more knowledgeable about financial matters than Peter. His biggest and best attribute is his devotion to charity. To list the endeavors Peter is and has been involved in would require its own book. He always tells it like it is unlike the talking heads you hear on TV and other media. If you have any thoughts on working with Peter, don't hesitate. You are working with one fine honest and capable man.

S.S. – Manalapan, NJ

Peter is straightforward, honest, and trustworthy. His opinions and predictions are spot on . There is no second thinking or second guessing. He backs his statements up with facts and experience and that gives all who do business with Peter a sense of relief and confidence – especially in these uncertain times. Highly recommend!!

J.B.M. – Freehold, NJ

When it comes to finance and questions about the economy, I have found no better source than Peter Grandich. Straight to the point, honest and dependable, Peter has been "on the money" whenever I have sought his advice. I'd recommend anyone take the time to chat with Peter and see how his team can help you.

G.D. – Colts Neck, NJ

I have been following you for almost 20 years. I remember watching you on BNN with Jim O'Connell so many years ago. I appreciate your honesty and integrity. Until about 10 years ago, I was never a religious person. Following you has helped me understand the importance of believing. I now pray and or thank Jesus every day.

I thank you for the guidance you've given me in the markets all these years but more importantly guidance to realize there's more to life than the markets and money.

T.A. – Vancouver, Canada

Peter Grandich and his team have been fantastic for my wife and I as we plan financially for our future. They've always been available to answer any and all questions we've had and made us feel very comfortable. Extremely trustworthy and someone I'd recommend to everyone.

T.W. – Point Pleasant, NJ

Made in USA - North Chelmsford, MA
1330663_9798841164708
09.06.2022 1803